Henry Bagshaw

Diatribae

Discourses upon Select Texts

Henry Bagshaw

Diatribae
Discourses upon Select Texts

ISBN/EAN: 9783337346126

Printed in Europe, USA, Canada, Australia, Japan

Cover: Foto ©Thomas Meinert / pixelio.de

More available books at **www.hansebooks.com**

DIATRIBÆ;

O·R

Diſcourſes

U P O N

SELECT TEXTS:

Wherein
Several weighty Truths are handled
and applyed againſt the

PAPIST

AND THE

SOCINIAN·

By *HENRY BAGSHAW*, D. D.

L O N D O N,
Printed by *T. H.* for *Ric. Chiſwell* at the *Roſe*
and *Crown* in St. *Paul's Churchyard,* 1680.

TO

The Right Honourable and
Reverend Father in God,

Nathaniel,

Lord Biſhop of *Durham*.

My Lord,

I *Have been long doubtful in my thoughts what Sub-jects to handle under ſo great a variety of Chriſtian Truths; but I do not doubt in the leaſt where I ſhould fix my Dedication ; ſince your Lordſhip may challenge*

*all my endeavours, whether I
be barely conſider'd as a* Member *of your* Dioceſs *, or farther as* planted *by your ſelf
under the noble* Influence *of
your* Favour. *As a* Member,
there is due from me all the
Reverence *of an* Eſteem : *as
one* planted, *there is requiſite
the peculiar* tribute *of a* thank-
ful mind *in a return of ſome*
Fruit *to your hands.*

The Diſcourſes *I here offer
to your* Lordſhips *view, and
from thence to the* World
(how weakly *ſoever they are
written) yet* I *am ſure they
have* weight *of* matter *and
worth of* Patronage *to defend
them.*

them. I here open from Scripture, *Firft,that heynous fin of* Imprifoning Truth, *and the juftnefs of Gods vengeance reveal'd* : *Next, the natural Inference from* Divine Promifes, *which is the exercife of all* Piety : *Thirdly, the cogent reafon of adhering to our* Lord Chrift, *becaufe* He *has* words of Eternal life *for his followers* : *Laft of all, the proper* Benefit *of his* Death *in that work of* Juftifying *us, and the* Peculiar *Advantages of his* Rifing : *In all which points I have ftrictly confin'd my felf within my* Circle; *and (as occafion led me) reflected upon*

Two

Two great Enemies *to* Chriftianity, *which are the* Papift *and the* Socinian; *the one crying up his* Diana (*which is* the Church) *the other magnifying as* falfe *a* Goddefs (*which is* his own Reafon) *to overthrow it.*

I need not here publifh your Lordfhips Zeal *for our* Proteftant Church, *which you have abundantly* demonftrated *to your own* Clergy, *nor the* prudence *of your* Government, *which we all* tafte *of: but fince* I *am made fo fingular an* Inftance *of your* kindnefs *both as to* prefent *and future encouragement,* I *take leave to mention*

tion it to the world, and withall to acquaint your Lordſhip,
That the great Temptation I
had to write was my Senſe of
it; where I hoped I might e-
rect ſome laſting Memorial; or
(if the poorneſs of what is
written ſhould hinder life,) yet
the Candid Reader might
give it one by conſidering your
Lordſhips Name, and the Gratitude of the Writer.

I am, my Noble Lord,

Houghton le ſpring,　Your Lordſhips
Sept. 30. 1679.

Moſt obliged and ever

faithful Servant,

Henry Bagshaw.

The Firſt Diſcourſe.

Rom. 1. 18.

For the wrath of God is revealed from Heaven againſt all ungodlineſs and unrighteouſneſs of men, who hold the truth in unrighteouſneſs.

Theſe words have reference to the ſixteenth verſe of the Chapter, wherein the Apoſtle ſtoutly defends the Charge of his Miniſtry, becauſe the *Goſpel* he preached, though it might ſeem to have a weak Subject (*a Cruci-fied Saviour*) and as weak a Deli-verer of that Subject (*a deſpiſed Meſſenger*) yet was *the Power of God to Salvation.* How it prov'd ſuch an effectual Inſtrument in Gods

A   hands

hands to convert the World, He farther illuſtrates by the Methods and Rules of it, as being a *full revelation* of his Will, both to accept the imperfect righteouſneſs of men, and to puniſh their wilful diſobedience. In the one it ſutes it ſelf to our *higheſt Hopes*, by that *bleſſed Life* it propounds; in the other it is applied to our *greateſt Fears*, by that *curſed Death* it threatens : ſo that none can poſſibly eſcape the force of Religion, except at the ſame time their own paſſions be deſtroyd.

Now what is Gods rule of ſaving men by, he tells us in the Verſe foregoing my Text; and with what clearneſs of diſcovery the Goſpel lays open the *Juſtification* of a Sinner, and *Faith* the condition preſcribed : but leſt this Faith ſhould be miſtaken (as if Heaven were the reward of a naked

ked Belief, and a bare relyance on
Chrift might buy out his purchafe)
he checks our confidence by another Manifeftation of Gods Juftice
againft Sinners, As *the Juft shall live
by Faith*, (whereby He means Faith
that is the Principle of a new life,)
fo the Wicked fhall die for their
Impenitence; and both thefe ftates
the ·Gofpel reveals; a *Light* fent
us from above to work *doubly* upon Earth, in *refreshing* the Saint,
and *confuming* the Malefactor. *For
the wrath of God, &c.*

Whether the fcope of thefe
words be directed againft the *Gentiles*, who were fuch Rebels to *Na=
ture*, or againft a mungrel fort of
them (the *Gnofticks*) who were fuch
corrupters of the *Gofpel*, I fhall not
here examine, but confider them
barely in themfelves as they point
out to us a General Truth, which
is this,

The First Discourse.

That the wrath of God against all kind of sin, but especially the sin of those who hold the Truth in Unrighteousness, is plainly discovered in the Gospel.

In the management of this Truth it will be necessary to enquire into these particulars.

1. Into the Nature of Gods Wrath, what it implyes.

2. Why the Revelation of his Wrath is more peculiarly ascrib'd to the Gospel?

3. How justly it is exercised upon those Sinners who hold the Truth in Unrighteousness.

I. Into the Nature of Gods *Wrath,* what it implyes.

The holy Pen-men of Scripture that borrowed our Passions to express the manner of Gods dealing with us, teach us withal to abstract from the weakness of them. Passions in us shew the imperfectness

of

of our beings, that we need ſuch *Principles* to act by ; and the imperfectneſs too of our State, in that Trouble follows their *Motion*: And particularly this paſſion of *Wrath* is attended with a double one ; either if you regard the diſturbance it raiſes in the Soul upon the ſenſe of an Injury, or the poor limiting of it to Time in its effects of puniſhing: in neither ſenſe can it belong to God ; for could He be diſturbed when provok'd, He would loſe the *Happineſs of his State* ; could He be limited in his Vengeance, He would loſe the *Glory of his Power*.

Therefore his Wrath in this place can ſignifie nothing elſe but a ſettled decree, or fixt will of puniſhing ſin eternally. This is a revenge proper to God, and it is this alone makes the Tranſgreſſor fear : In this ſenſe it is taken by

.A 3   *John*

John the Baptist, when he warns his hearers to *flee from the Wrath to come*; and by St. *Paul* when he speaks of *the day of Wrath*; styl'd so with an Emphasis, to distinguish it from Gods other days of Execution in this world.

Here a Day of Justice may rather be termed *Night* for its darknefs, and Providence it self seems to be clouded even in those *Thunderbolts* that come down; but the Day wherein the sinners eternal Portion will be assigned, is a clear one; for it derives its distinguishing light from the scorching *Flame* that *preys* on him. Did not God thus punish the Offender, all his other Judgments would not bridle us, nor could there be a sufficient Evidence of his wrath, did it only *light* on the party, but not *stay nor abide* on him : Then Justice appears to be his, when it is not

com-

common with man's; but man can temporally punish and be mocked to by the Sufferer, since that Death he inflicts as his highest punishment, is but an end and escape from it. Wee all foolishly burn in our wrath, and the fires we prepare for othes carry a vain heart in them; they *scorch and heal together*, they dissolve the body to ashes, and *cool* it by doing so; but when Eternal Wrath seizes on us, when Everlasting Burnings break forth, this is to give the *substance* of pain, and no *shadows*. In this way God rewards mens evil deads, and by the terror of it keeps his infinite mercy from being abused; which is an Attribute that wicked men naturally stick to, and as hardly quit their hold of it in pursuit of their wickedness, were they not shaken off by another notion of Infinite Justice.

. proceed to my ſecond Query,
II Why the Revelation of Divine Wrath is peculiarly aſcribed
to the Goſpel ? This is intimated
in my Text ; *For the wrath of God*
(ſayes the Apoſtle) *is revealed from*
Heaven, that is immediately by
the God of it, who deſcended upon earth to teach the world , and
in an heavenly manner confirmed
what He taught , ſealing by his
Works the Truths He delivered.

In handling this point I ſhall
premiſe two things, which are here
neceſſarily imply'd.

1. That the eternal puniſhment
of evil doers was a Truth decreed ·
by God, before it was *revealed* :
for Revelation gives no *Eſſence*
to things , but only an *Appearance*
to us : it is not a creating but a diſ-
covering work ; not a ſaying, let
it be, but let it be with full Evidence. He that opens the earth,

and

and produces thofe ftores it fhuts up, does not thereby caufe them to *exift*, but to be *known*; fo when Gods wrath is faid here to be manifefted, it imports this, That it was firft prepared. His decree was paft from all eternity againft fin; having determined with himfelf to create Man, and govern him by Law, determin'd likewife a Punifhment anfwerable to the Majefty of the Lawgiver; from whofe infinity Mans guilt fhould fwell up, fo as to deferve infinite Wages.

The Wrath then of God was fure before-hand; only the benefit we have by his revealing it is the applying of that Truth to us, whereby we are warned to feek out and provide a remedy of the Judgment.

2. The fecond thing I fhall premife is, That till the Gofpel came

came, the nature of Gods Vindictive Juftice was much hid and
concealed.

It is true the Gentiles had a
Light from Heaven (which was
the *Light of Nature* , *the Candle of
the Lord*) and the Jews a more fpe-
cial one, which was the *Light of
the Law* to direct them ; yet neither of them contained a like evidence of this Truth which the
Gofpel affords us.

1. For the Light of Nature the
Gentiles were led by ;

I confefs they had unalterably
this dictate from it, that *Wrath* was
the due pay of Offenders; and be=
caufe men liv'd not up to the
Principles of their Creation, they
were therefore juftly lyable to the
Curfe ; but how far that Judgment fhould certainly extend,
herein the Light fail'd to guide
them. Reafon it felf taught them to
con-

conclude the Wicked deſerv'd puniſhment; but the Reaſon did not
ſuffice to confirm that puniſhment
in another World; for how Man
could eternally ſubſiſt in a courſe
of miſery they underſtood not,
nor what conſiſtency there was of
an immortal being with perpetual
Torments πᾶν Ἰὸ ἀλγὲν θνῖἸὸν ἐσι was the
Speech of one of their chief Philoſophers; as if to *Suffer* and to
be *Mortal* were one and the ſame
thing.

I need not mention the groſneſs
of their miſtakes about the Nature
of him they worſhipped, which is
palpable to all from that Idolatry
they invented; but their Error al=
ſo is alike notorious as to thoſe
Motives they fail'd in, for urging
Religion upon men. For when
they denied the *Reſurrection* of the
Body as *Impoſſible*, they muſt con-
ſequently deny an *Eternal Reward*

that

that was built on it. What we
read in the *Acts* to be the profeſt
Mockery of the Epicureans and Sto-
icks (when St. *Paul* preached to
them upon this Theme) was indeed the *ſport* of all the reſt; who
ſcoff'd at any thing above Nature,
and minding only the conſtant
courſe of its operations, made ac-
cordingly their Eſtimate of Gods
Power. But perhaps they deliver'd ſomewhat concerning the
Life of the *Soul* ; but then they
did it very uncertainly (as *Socrates*
in his Apology for himſelf before
his Judges ſufficiently witneſſes)
and if any of them were ſo poſitive
as to affirm it, yet they made that
ſtate after death ſo Aery and ſo Ro-
mantick, that neither the Juſt man
could be refreſh'd, nor the Wicked
frighted with that opinion.

Go to their Stories of the *Dark
Regions* below , and the *Fiery Lake*
the

the Bad ſhould be caſt into ; *the Stone*, *the Wheel and the Vulture* that was appointed them ; theſe were the reports of their *Poets*, ſit *Prieſts* for ſuch Worſhip= pers. Little did they work upon mens Faiths to believe them, who with their fabulous mixtures cor- rupting Truth, hindred thereby the conviction of their Hearers. Hence their great ones were not mov'd with what was related to them ; and the Vulgar did but conſider them as *Tragedies* upon a *Stage* ; where Fears perhaps were raiſ'd in them from the Appre- henſion of an Evil, and again eaſily cur'd with the conceit of a Fiction. In a word whatever Religion they had concerning another life , it was made by Fancy a wild Specu- lation, and had no check upon conſcience to bind practice ; ſo that to them the Wrath of God here

here in my Text prov'd ftill a
Doctrine unknown.

2. Let us examine the Doctrin
of the Jews, and that Light of
Special Revelation. which they
enjoyed.

It muft be granted by all Chriftians, that the Jews had their
Covenant eftablifhed upon promifes and threatnings of an Eternal
Condition. God who chofe them
out 'of all Nations to be his People, and govern'd their State peculiarly by his Laws, did by this
too diftinguifh them from the reft
of the World, that they had their
Religion advanced by thofe Prophets He fent amongft them:
whence we find it vindicated by
Chrift in a *Difpute*, by *Paul* in a
Defence, by *Abraham* in a *Parable*.
Chrifts proves from thence his
Doctrine of the *Refurrection*, *Paul*
his *hope of the Promife*, and *Abraham*
the

the *different ſtate both of good and bad* ; which one would think were e-nough to ſtop the mouths of our *Modern Saduccees* when the *Old* were put to *ſilence.* And indeed who= ever ſhall aſſert that the Jews had no ſuch benefit of Revelation, he muſt at once charge their *Lawgi-ver* with *weakneſs* , and their own *Faith* with *abſurdity* in cleaving to him.

Yet however, this Law of the Jews (if compared with the Chri= ſtian in the manner of its evidence) came not up to the excellency of that diſcovery. For the whole *Moſaïck* Oeconomy was made up of *Types and Figures* , and a thick *Night* continually overſpread their *Tabernacle* : Their *Promiſes* and *Cur= ſes* literally concerned the things of this life, and it required a pier-cing Faith *ſpiritually* to interpret them : a vulgar eye would ſurely

ſtay

ſtay upon the Surface; but for to be able to take in the depth, this muſt proceed from a ſtrong en-lightning, which we read only a few were bleſt with, that like *Moſes* were carried up to ſee the-hidden things of the *Mount*, when the generality ſtood below and ſaw nothing but *Clouds*.

There was then great need of a Saviour to appear, whether we regard Jew or Gentile; and that not only for the work of *ſaving Man-kind*, but *for redeeming Truth*, which was ſo obſcur'd by the one, and loſt by the other. Now Chriſt has diſcharg'd his Office in this parti=cular; and for this *Prophet* alone was reſerv'd all the glory of Di-vine Revelation, who being *the expreſs Image of his Fathers Perſon*, was the Signifier alſo of his *Will* in the brighteſt Character.

We

We know in the Creation *Light* was Gods *first work*, but in reftoring of Religion his *last*·He judg'd it not fit to bring bright day on his People at firft, but by degrees to prepare their weak fight that it might be the better confirm'd ; and when the full time came, the Gofpel was publifhed, which put an end to farther difcoveries and feal'd up the Vifion.

·This being premif'd, it remains I fhould fpeak one word to fhew how *Gods wrath* by way of eminency is revealed in the *Gofpel* : which will appear by confidering,

1. The Cleernefs of it in the Letter.

2. The Publick Promulgation of it to the World.

1. For the Clearnefs of the Letter ; nothing can be more lively fhown than the Sinners Hell, whofe *Worm* is faid *not to dye* ; neither

B ther

ther is his *Fire quenched* : Nor does
the *Second Death* ceafe from *hurting*
him.   Should we now conclude
with the *Socinian*, Eternal Punifhment to be nothing elfe but Per-
dition or a Negation of Exiftence,
we muft flatly deny thofe phrafes
of Scripture before mentioned;
for the *Worm* it felf dies if its *prey*
does fo ; the *Fire* is put out if the
matter it feeds upon be not lafting;
and the *Second Death* is not in the
leaft hurtful, if it imply nothing
of *torment.*   But befides (were this
granted them) what's become of
the fiercenefs of Gods wrath, when
neither felt nor endured ? Where
is his Judgment and fevere rec-
koning with evil doers , if they
partake with Brutes in their end?
It is folly to fear where Juftice is
not known; and confequently a
wide gap is opened by fuch men
to all impiety, when they take off
the

the Terrors of Death, leaving men
as unconcern'd to be nothing an
hundred years hence, as an hundred years paſt to be unborn. O
the *vanity* of that *Reaſon* they pretend to, which breaks the Authority of Gods Laws ! O the *cruelty*
of their *Compaſſion* to Mans nature,
whereby Religion it ſelf is deſtroy'd ! But Chriſt has otherwiſe
inſtruĉted the World,and knowing
it needful that *Everlaſting Puniſhment* ſhould be equally ſet before
us with *Life Eternal* ; He has joyned them both in the Sentence, that
we might be every way convinc'd
Eternity is our lot, and therefore
a full motive to Duty.

In the Old Teſtament *Tophet* or
the Valley of the Children of *Hin-
nom* (where their Sons and Daughters were ſacrificed to *Moloch*)
·was uſed by the Prophet *Iſaiah* as
his greateſt Type and Repreſenta-

tion of Hell: But how ſhort it fell
of a Goſpel-deſcription will be
made evident, if we conſult the
place, the *number* it was prepared
for, and the *time* of its burning :
the *place* though deep, yet had
bottom : the *number* though great,
yet was *limited to one People*; and
the *time* of its burning though
fierce, yet had *end*. On the contrary the Goſpel reveals a *bottom-*
leſs Gulf, a *multitude of all Nations*
that enter, and a *perpetual duration*
of their torments. So that here we
have a clear light of the Letter,
wherein the Jews were defective.

Neither does the excellency of
a Revelation ſtop here, but we
may conſider in the ſecond place :

2. The Publick Promulgation
of it to the World; and the *Seal*
it carries of an *Univerſal Publiſhing*,
anſwerable to the *Majeſty* of him ·
that came to ſet up an *Univerſall*
                                    King-

Kingdom. Behold, the Sentence of
Divine Wrath was before hid with
the Jews; but now the knowledg of it ſpreads into all parts,
and ſo it proves a new Light in
regard of its extent through all
quarters. That *Sun of righteouſneſs,*
that has riſen, ſhines round about,
not only *with healing under his wings
to preſerve,* but with *Flames* too of
vengeance to *conſume.* And this
He manifeſted here on Earth,
when he proclaimed the Glad-ty-
dings of Salvation, and pronounc'd
many a Bleſſing upon his People;
yet left they ſhould forget the Juſtice of a Saviour, *Woes* and *Threat-*
nings were uſhered in, to allay
and temper all his Miniſtry.
Therefore thoſe that heard him,
had reaſon to fear, and not think
themſelves freed from *Legal terrors,*
ſince the *Thunder* of *Sinai* continued
ſtill, though the *Darkneſs* of it was
gone. B 3 And

And as He thus awed them with his own Teaching, ſo He commiſſioned his Servants to do likewiſe, when He ſent them abroad to teach all Nations. Mercy alone was not their Theme, nor the riches of Divine Grace in mans Redemption (which is ſuch welcome news to the receiver) but the Curſe was alſo annext, and the Charge of future Judgment; that if the former did pleaſe, the latter might bind. Before this, *Ignorance* might be ſome way pleaded by the Gentiles, that they obeyed not Gods Law, when Life and Immortality were not known; but after theſe were cleared up in the Goſpel, then their Condemnation was perfected. For now they could be no longer termed unhappy for ſitting in *Darkneſs* and in the *Shadow of Death*, which is a kind of Sanctuary to the Pleader, but

but Wicked for *loving* the Shadow which is the beginning of Hell. Upon this account He no more *winks* or ſpares, but *judicially eying* their ſteps, denounces againſt them his heavieſt Judgment.

I know many refer the Revelation of Gods Wrath to the Experiments of it in the world, and make his outward Judgments upon ſinners as ſo many Witneſſes to confirm it. But were no higher meant than thoſe Inſtances, we ſhould be ſtill in the dark; convinc'd perhaps he was wroth, but not wroth to a diſtinction, wherein Juſtice is revealed. None can ſpell out *Characters* of Providence, nor read the ſpecial *Hand=writing* upon the *Wall* without the benefit of *Viſion.* What is all our ſight of a juſt God here but ἐν αἰνίγμαλι in a Riddle, a Riddle that has buſied Philoſophers to reſolve, and hardned their

doubts

doubts by the enquiry ? If Wrath
be manifeſted, let the bad feel its
burden; but alas! Gods Tempeſts
here·ſeem onely to fall upon his
own Chóſen : They may call it
Grace thus to ſuffer, but it is *Grace*
not ſeen, nor acknowledged by o-
thers, all the *face* of it being ſpoil'd
in the *Storm.*

On the other ſide the calm and
luſtre of outward good, this is generally the wicked mans ſhare;
we may call it *Puniſhment* thus to
flouriſh, but it is a *Puniſhment de-*
ſired. Now to break up the *Pit*
and ſhew thoſe Treaſures of vengeance ſhut up there; to ſearch
into a wicked mans Fate, and diſ-
cover the Miſeries that follow it;
to repreſent him naked in his
Grave, and awak'd afterwards in
that nakedneſs for ſcourging, this
is properly to reveal Wrath, and
to the Goſpel we muſt owe ſuch a
Diſcovery.   Thus

Thus much for my Second Particular. There remains the Third to discuss, which is this.

III. How justly it is exercised upon those who hold the Truth in Unrighteousnels?

In discussing this Head I shall first open the *Charge*, and then it will be easie to prove the justness of the *Sentence*.

The *Charge* laid against the Sinner is not *error* of mind, nor *weakness* of passion, nor *decay* of nature (which are Guilt attended with an Apology) but the *tyranny* of a *corrupt heart* ; That hating the Empire of *Truth*, takes it *prisoner* to be freed from its Government : for so the word κατέχειν properly signifies , namely forcibly to withhold or detain Truth, that is, to obstruct the power of Religion.

What a high piece of injustice
this

this is, will be evidenc'd if you regard,

1. The Act in it ſelf.
2. The Motives that lead
   men to it.
3. The Effects that flow
   from it.

1. As to the Act; it is no leſs
than the ſeizure of a *Soveraign
Prince*; for ſuch *Truth*, is; and
therefore juſtly demands to have
Juriſdiction in the ſoul, and like
Light to ſpread in its full liberty.
What have Subjects to do with
fettering Princes, whom they are
bound to obey, or keeping them
in the dark when they ought to be
viſible in the Throne ? Kings are
only at *Babylon* led captive : There
they have *their eyes put out , and
their feet bound,* that they can neither ſee nor walk abroad : So the
Chriſtian Law (that ought to rule
in the World) is at *Rome* barba=
rouſly

roufly ufed ; a place eminent for *kindling* of *Lamps*, and for *fmother-ing* of *Light* ; for *adorning* of *Altars*, and for *corrupting* the *Sacrifice*. What I befeech you is all their Worfhip but *blind and lame*, Truth being fo ill rack'd with their handling, that they can only ac-quaint us with the deformities of its body ? The *Prifon* it fuffers in is that of *One Language*, hardly re-vealed to the Priefts themfelves ; the *Eyes* it has are thofe Figur'd ones of an *Idoll*, that need the gildings of Art to be own'd : the *Feet* are the fupports of a *Tradition* which requires an *Implicit Faith*, that is, Faith of the fame *lamenefs*. Who that fees Truth in this fhape will not fay it is vilify'd by its profeffors, when the bare with-holding it from others is a high Act of Injuftice ? For that Act is a withholding of the Birth-right

and

and Inheritance of Men, and a frustrating of Gods purpose in the gift of it ; who as he has design'd the *Elements of Nature* to be commonly enjoyed for our *Bodily* sustentation, so he has also design'd the *Elements of Truth* to be with a like commonness imparted for preserving the *Soul.*

Yet these kind of men (that lead Scripture captive) dare plead the *Infallibility* of their own Church ; a word wherein *the Mystery of Iniquity* is sum'd up, and from whence they have fetcht all their *Artillery* to beat down every thing that oppofed them : which puts me in mind of that famous Engine *Demetrius* contriv'd, and is mentioned by *Plutarch* in his Life, that had several Rooms and Partitions in it to hold Souldiers ; and the men that lodg'd there did fight with all forts of weapons. Such is their

their *Engine* of an *Infallible Guide*;
but certainly of it self it would
little prevail, were it not for its
many *Cells* and the Forces that fill
them. For behold! what Bands
of *Friers*, what Companies of
Priests lie there arm'd and pre-
par'd to defend their Cause! This
word (*Infallible*) has strength e-
nough with them to solve all Arguments for *Truth*, to remove all
objections against *Error*; and withall it so blinds their whole party,
that they can neither discern any
compounded mixtures in Faith,
nor notorious scandals in practice;
though the one proceeds from all
the grosness of *Humane Invention*,
and the other from all the licen-
tiousness of *Corrupt Nature*.

But the falseness of that Title
they pretend to, is sufficiently laid
open in the world; and they themselves too might be convinc'd of
the

the arrogance of their claim; ſince what-ever promiſe they may plead for ſuch an aſſiſtance, con= cerns only the *leading* of the *Uni-verſal Church*, and is limited too in its ſenſe to points *neceſſary for its ſalvation*; whereas they (being on-ly a *part* of that Body, and a part wretchedly *fallen* in Chriſtian Prin= ciples) cannot truly be ſaid to be upheld by the *Spirit*, but rather Judicially forſaken, by reaſon of their baniſhing the *Word of Truth*, which can only ſecure the Spirits Conduct. But I paſs from hence to the Second Aggravation of this ſin; wherein I ſhall conſider,

2. The Motives that lead men to it.

Could men urge ſome power-ful Temptation for the reaſon they had to hinder *the Authority of Religion* over them, they might fetch an excuſe from it; but when
a baſe

a baſe luſt, a ſordid appetite ſhall get ſtrength to prevail, this heightens the Crime becauſe of the ſhamefulneſs of that Conqueſt. In all Irreligion we are poorly maſter'd, or rather betray'd. The Will quits its allegiance to the Underſtanding (which by nature it is a ſervant to) for a mean, narrow, ſhrunken object, that cannot ſo much as bribe it by a Reward. Atheiſm is built upon groſs dictates of *Senſe*, and *Luſt* forms to its ſelf principles to reſiſt *Conſcience*; wherein Man (pretending to live free) is left miſerably bound by his *Slave*. Conſult the whole Method of an Atheiſtical diſcourſe: In Fleſh it begins and ends with it; but take once out of Mans mind *carnal Hopes*, and *ſenſual Ima=ginations*, then the Soul comes to do it ſelf right, by being filled with proper Ideas of God and Eternity.

Devo-

Devotion is the genuine birth of our Thoughts while the streams of them are pure; but Impiety is a *Monster*, that out of *mud and slime* is formed. We may know its O-riginal by its Fruits, and the de-bauchery of an Atheist's reason by his practice, whose love of Drink, Whoredom, Gluttony, and other foul Uncleannesses, furnishes him with Arguments to defend them. Upon the same score the Heathens maintain'd their Idol-Temples, because their inclinations led them to vice, and the Gods of those Temples showed them the way.

The like Reason may be given for that exact care and diligence in the *Roman*-Church to suppress Truth, which is *Lust* and *Interest*. These are the Two commanding Principles they are sway'd by, and *Unrighteousness* is serv'd by them for low wages. They hide the

the true doctrine of a *preſent Re=pentance*, that their followers may ſin all their life-time without fear, and at laſt purge by *Confeſſion* : They conceal the True Tenet of Chriſts *full ſatisfaction* (whereby both ſin and puniſhment are taken off) that they may make an *Ex=chequer* of Mans Pardons : They deſtroy the nature of *Good Works*, and make them to be nothing elſe but an *Art* of *Compounding* : The *Creature* is ſet up by them (as it was by the *Gentiles*) παρὰ τὸν κτίσαντα *beſides the Creator* : They drive at *Univerſal Empire* and Soveraignty, and in order to this all *worldly Stratagems* are made uſe of ; ſo that it is hard to judg whether their *Capitol* or their *Church* be better founded. A *Mans Head* (we know) did denominate the one , and I am ſure it lies at the *Foundation* of the other ; except you'l ſay the *Old Serpent*

C   gets

gets in to help the *Subtilty* of it, and to mix his *poyſon* with the Invention. Indeed they may boaſt of their Politicks thus improv'd. But whoever will ſurvey the whole Model of their Religion, or impartially view their Diſcipline and Practice, he ſhall find Truth is hid by them for carnal ends, which adds new height to the ſin.

3. The third and laſt aggravation is drawn from the effects that follow this violence offer'd to Truth.

Whoever ſhall ſuppreſs the power of Religion in himſelf, does thereby contract a hardneſs in his ſoul to commit iniquity, and lives a continued ſcandal to his Brethren; but whoſoever ſhall ſuppreſs *Truth* by a Law, he thereby proclaims his defiance of it, and employes all his force to fix Error and Corruption in the World. How can

can Injuſtice riſe higher than this
caſe! for it is a *flat war againſt Hea=*
ven ; a *publick Invaſion of each mans*
privilege; it is a *digging of the Eyes*
out of that *Head*, which ſhould be
general in its shine ; and a reducing of
things to a *ſtrange Chaos* ; where
the confuſion is far worſe (when
Truth and Falſehood, Good and
Evil are not known) than when
Heaven and Earth lay undiſtingui-
ſhed. O how ſad and deplorable is
Mens caſe, to be left in ignorance
of their way to Eternal Happineſs!
Who can poſſibly attain to Life
without a knowledge of it before
hand, or be brought *from the power*
of Satan unto God, except their *eyes*
be firſt opened, and their Spiritual
Blindneſs removed? There is no
altering of Gods Methods to ſave,
nor of the courſe of his Spirit to convert men; who begins in an act of
Conviction upon the Underſtanding,

and conveys by it to the Will its *ſanĉtifying operation* ; ſo that without *enlightning* there can be no *renewing* of the inner man, and by conſequence no fitting or preparing of him for Glory. So then look where Truth is hid, there ſo many ſouls are buried, and deſcend by degrees from one Gulf into another. Till the Priſon be broke, and light again reſtored, a recovery is impoſſible. Therefore when ſuch a *General ruine* is the iſſue of *Religions Captivity*, the crime of detaining it muſt needs be heinous, and ariſe in proportion to thoſe miſchiefs that are cauſed.

I could alledg the ſame inſtance I before mentioned, as a pregnant proof to ſhew how deſtructive it is to a people that *Truth* ſhould be withheld, and an *Inquiſition* eſtabliſhed to keep off that Tryal. Hence multitudes periſh for lack of of Knowledg, and wanting a requisite Faith (which a blind Credulity takes the place of) are in all the folly of it condemn'd. But *light* they pretend wounds men, and Scripture (if publick) deceives, many wresting it to their own destruction; a liberty (say they) of Christian knowledg is but a Curse and a *rank Field* for several *Heresies* to spring up; whence it is better to root it out, and thereby hinder the growth of tares. But an Objection of this kind is easily answered: for there was never any thing of great esteem and use for mans Life, but it bred a difference in opinion. As Physick intended for the cure of Bodies, and Philosophy for the health of Souls, are both fruitful of many questions; yet none in his wits would avoid Physick or Philosophy, because of *different Sects and Parties* they breed;

C 3   so

fo neither fhould *the free use of Scripture* be condemned, in regard of *differences* amongft men; which proceed not fo much from their ftudy of contention, as from a va= riety in their abilities to under- ftand. Farther, were this charge of theirs valid to null the force of the rule, let then the great *Eye* of the *Firmament* be pulled out, becaufe he raifes *vapours* as well as *enlight- ens*: The *vapours* that are rais'd he owes to the *Earth*, but *enlightning* muft be afcrib'd to *his own Body*. Would we certainly know the rea- fon why the Gofpel is hid? It is jealoufie and fear of being refor- med: An evil eye will not bear Light, nor a difeafed Confcience retain it: Light reproves and con= vinces where it comes; for this caufe they keep it clofe, dealing with Truth as the *Tyrians* did with their God, whom they fetter'd with

with a ſtrong *Chain*, left (if free) he
ſhould leave their *City*, and take
the *Enemies ſide*.

Hitherto I have ſpoken of the
Charge; whoſe greatneſs does ap=
pear from the treaſon that is in the
Act, from the baſeneſs of the motives, and from the murdering nature of the effects : proceed we to
ſpeak a little of the juſtneſs of the
Sentence that is here denounced a=
gainſt thoſe who hold the Truth
in Unrighteouſneſs.

It may perhaps be counted a
diſproportionable reward by ſome,
that wicked mens *finite Acts* ſhould
be *everlaſtingly* puniſhed : but did
they farther regard them as *Acts
of Strength* where the *Will* governs,
Acts of Enmity where *Revelation is
oppoſ'd*, they would not ſo readily
complain of the *rigour* of that
Judgment. Beſides there is an ab-
ſolute neceſſity for ſuch a *Sentence*

to

to secure Religion in the World, since the bounds of Christianity would be quickly past over, were not *infinite terrors* the fence to keep Travellers in. And what seems more loudly to call for it, than the sin I have already discours'd of? or how shall the authority of Truth be maintain'd, the honour of God vindicated, and the injuries done to our Brethren aveng'd, but by so signal a punishment? Take thy measures of the offence from the Object: in that Glass thou mayst discern its full stature. He that quenches *Light*, strives to destroy the God of it; which being so high a provocation, the same God is sollicited to exercise his Omnipotence in a revenge. The Princes of this World would be satisfied to the utmost, when their Subjects daringly rebel; only their want of power causes a weaknefs

in

in their blows : God that can take the extremity of a payment when an affront is offer'd him, purſues but the will of a Soveraign in do= ing ſo.

Did he indeed hide Truth from us, we might likewiſe be hid from his Juſtice : but when he clearly propounds it to us, and enables our Wills to cloſe with it, here we inexcuſably offend. Now we ſay *we ſee*, therefore *our ſin remains;* now we confeſs we are aſſiſted by Heaven, therefore Heaven is *ab- ſolv'd* when it puniſhes. May we not with ſhame own that reproof which God delivered againſt *Iſrael, Your deſtruction is of your ſelves?* May we not apply what he had ſpoken againſt *Jeruſalem, What could have been done more for my Vineyard that was not done?* For he has taught us by his *Word*, awakened us by his *Rod*, invited us by his *Bounty*, of= fered

fered himself to us by his *Grace*, while we desperately forsake our own mercy. Even the worst of men taste of his Goodness; They find his Spirit in their *Consciences* to check, in their *Minds* to guide, in their *Wills* to allure them; he wooes, he sollicits, he waits, all our Faculties he besets, that he might draw us over to the Government of his Laws. He is always free and communicative of his Treasures, but it is mans guilt cuts off the spring. Tax not then the Method of Gods proceedings, that summons into an extraordinary Court the gross abuser of his Talents; but reflect sadly upon the sinfulness of thine own ways, that causes *Grace* to alter its *shape*, and the *face* of a *Saviour* to be *transfigur'd* with *darkness*.

I shall close this point with an Inference from the whole.

I suppofe none will expect in this place I fhould attempt a defcription of *Divine Wrath*, which though it be revealed from Heaven, is yet hid in the manner of execution. So *Lightning* is difcerned by its *brightnefs* when it ftrikes, though the way of its working is not feen. How the *Fire* below by an Almighty breath will be kindled, and yet kept by the fame breath from confuming the Sinner, it is not for us to explain; but certainly the Wound, the Smart, the Plague is intolerable, where-ever the weight of Gods Juftice falls. And they of all men will feel its burden, that bring Light to their punifhment; whereby they are forced to acknowledge the *double calamity* they are preft with, namely *Wrath* not to be *fhunn'd*, and *Sin* not to be *pleaded for.* Here the *Sword* cuts deep, enters the very marrow and
spirits,

spirits, and *renews* continually its *edge with piercing*. Who is able to meet Vengeance in its affaults, and Light in its convictions? Is not their force ftrong, nay irrefiftible where they come? Behold! the one *makes*, and the other *quickens* our Hell; the one *binds* us faft, and the other *heats* our Furnace.

I know the Theme I now infift on is not fuited to a Scoffers ear, becaufe not fuited to his defigns. What have we to do (fays an Epicure) with a warning of Gods Juftice, that chaftifes all our delights, and mingles gall with our pleafures? If Religion muft be preached up, let Grace and Mercy be revealed · Thofe have a healing quality in them, and like *Beds of ſpices* refrefh with their *opening*; but Treafures of Wrath, and the Pains of another World, thefe like *noyfome pits* do punifh us in our *ſearch-*
ing.

ing. Thus he would secure his way of sinning to himself, and remove all sting from his conscience.

But alas! his arts are in vain; were he freed from any outward sounds of the Ministry of the Word, yet his mind is still checked with a future Judgment, and by fits submits to the Revelation. Indeed how can it be otherwise? for the notions of God and his Justice are twisted together in our Souls; and the same impression that convinces us of his Being, convinces us too of his Wrath against sin : nothing remains but that the eternity of it appear, and when that is effected, the Soul necessarily yields, and witnesses its surrender by those pungent acts of reflecting. ·

We suppose now adayes *Atheism* to abound, and fortifie that supposition by our frequent discourses to confute it; but if there be such

a *Le*-

a *Leproſie* amongſt Chriſtians , it
does not ſo much ſeize the *head* as
the *heart* , which is the *ſeat* of the
Devils Diſeaſe ; and he cares not
to ſpread it farther in his Children.
All our crime is, not that Divine
Characters in us are loſt, but only
hid in our ſouls : Truth we bury
by our practice, though we feel it
lives to our torment. And God
grant we be not puniſhed for our
Ingratitude with outward darkneſs
by a removal of his Candleſtick
from amongſt us. Do we now
pride our ſelves in this, that we
enjoy mercy ? but let us alſo regard the dangerous neighbour-
hood of Vindictive Juſtice, when
that Mercy is deſpiſ'd. What Attribute is there can reſcue us from
the ſtroke , when Goodneſs will
not defend ? Is it *Power* we may
flee to ? but that determines it ſelf
to deſtroy : Is it *Wiſdom* ? but that
con=

contrives the way of deſtroying : Is it *Holineſs* ? but that juſtifies the proceeding ; whence *Goodneſs* a-lone is the ſecurity of the Sinner : That *Altar of Refuge* God himſelf has ſet up to ſtop the courſe of his own Vengeance. And yet even here we are not ſafe, becauſe our abuſe forfeits the Privilege ; all the protection of it is loſt through our ſtubbornneſs of offending; whereby we become guilty of a *mad Sacrilege*, when we pull down the *Sanctuary* that might ſave us. There is no ſin ſo aggravating as what ſtrikes at God in an *Evange-lical* Revelation : for here we of-fend againſt his *laſt* and *beſt* method of drawing us to him.

You are all diggers in *Truths Mine*, and have your toyl paid with thoſe pleaſures you find there; but where ought it to be ſeen in its greateſt beauty, if not
    • amongſt

amongſt thoſe that chiefly diſco-
ver it? All kind of *Truth* has *charms*
upon its *face* to get Lovers, but
the *Truth of Religion* has a *Divine
Image* upon it to win Souls, and
an *Eternal Dowry* to hold them:
Blind are we if we reſiſt, abſurd
if we refuſe ſuch a Temptation.
The Duty I here preſs is very ſea-
ſonable; for the Object you ſee
deſerves Love, ay and the courage of Love to purſue it. How
can Luſts or Fears take room in a
Chriſtian, that has ſuch high Motives to govern him! Propound to
thy ſelf *Good and Evil* in their full
latitude here; ſwell them to their
biggeſt bulk; dreſs them in their
choiceſt colours and ſhows, they
ſink to nothing with a religious
compariſon: Heaven melts away
all the *paint* of a *preſent delight*, and
Hell renders all the *Vizards* of *outward danger* contemptible; ſo that

                                      neither

neither the one, nor the other, can ftir a paffion in the Soul when our thoughts are well planted.

Therefore if either the Mercy of a God can move, or the Wrath of Almighty can bind us ; if the Scepter of Grace can perfwade, or the Lightning of Juftice terrifie, if Life, if Death be of any moment to us, let us be faft maintainers of the *Truth*, and commend our Profeffion to the world by that *Infallible* ftamp of our lives.

D   The

---

2 Cor. 7. 1.

Having therefore theſe Promiſes , let us cleanſe our ſelves from all filthi-neſs both of Fleſh and Spirit, per-fecting Holineſs in the Fear of God.

IN the laſt verſe of the prece-ding Chapter (to which theſe words chiefly refer) we find what a gracious promiſe God makes to his People , when He aſſures them (if they ſeparate from ſin) in what a glorious manner He will receive them ; allowing them the nobleſt Privilege a Creature can have, and the beſt ſecurity to maintain it. For the Promiſe runs

D 2 thus,

thus, *I will be a Father unto you, and ye shall be my Sons and Daughters, saith the Lord Almighty*

Now the former of thefe Titles fpeaks not only the *nearnefs* of our *Creator*, but all the *bounty* of his *Grace* : the latter declares not only a *height* our *Natures* are raif'd to, but an equal *advancement* of our *Hopes* ; and the *Lord Almighty* (added in the clofe) is the beft *Security* againft *Fear*, fince a *Father* affuming it to himfelf, does thereby direct its influence to fave us.

I grant *Power* to be dreadful of it felf, and *Omnipotence* much more; but let the name of *Mercy* be joynd, all the pleafantnefs of its luftre is caft on it : we can then view it as a *calm Sea*, where breadth and depth grow delightful, by reafon of the gentlenefs of the Current : fo when an *Almighty Lord* confirms this to us, that He will treat us like

like *Sons*, we can then chearfully contemplate the Attribute of his Greatnefs, becaufe all the Majefty of it is allayed with his condefcend= ing goodnefs to Mankind. This then being every-where offered in the Gofpel (that perfect Model of Divine love) what is the Fruit we fhould return to our God, but fuch a work of obedience that pre= pares and fits us for what is pro-mifed; that ftamps upon us Gods Image in our Souls, and conveys with that Stamp our right to Glo-ry? *Having therefore thefe Promifes,* &c.

We may obferve in the words three particulars.

1. A Motive.
2. A Duty.
3. The Manner of perform-ing it.

The Motive anfwers our ut= moft defires; for it confifts of Di-vine *Promifes.* D 3 The

The Duty contains the beſt pre-
paratives; for it lies in purifying
of *Fleſh and Spirit.*

Laſtly, The Manner of performing it affords the ſureſt marks
to undeceive us; for it is a *Perfe=
cting of Holineſs in Gods Fear.*

The Firſt *perſwades*, the Second
qualifies, and the Third *diſtinguiſhes*
our Religion from the Worlds.

I begin with the *Motive*, as it
powerfully perſwades to Chriſtian
Practice: *Having therefore theſe Pro=
miſes* ---- Where we may note by
the way, how allowable it is in
our Chriſtian Profeſſion to regard
the Titles and Privileges of it for
the better encouragement of our
ſervice. It is not a *mercenary*, but a
rational act to eye a reward in any
action we perform; much more the
reward of eternal Bleſſedneſs; ſince
the very *End of our Faith* (with St.
Peter) is the *Salvation of our Souls.*

                              Moſes

Moses (the greateſt Prophet of the Jews, and a Type of our Lord Chriſt) had a reſpect to the *recompence* of reward; and this our Apoſtle St. *Paul* commands us in another place to *run that we may obtain*: ſo that to bid us do Gods Commandments meerly for the Beauty of Holineſs which is in them, without looking upon the Promiſes for our ſupport, is to make all our Religion a poor thin Speculation, when it affords us no proſpect; and to turn our Obedience into an uncomfortable ſlavery, by cutting off thoſe helps the Goſpel propounds for our Devotion.

But for the better handling of the Motive (here layd down) I ſhall conſider Two things.

1. The Nature of Mans will that is to be moved.

2. The fitneſs of Gods Promiſes to inflame it.

1. For

1. For the nature of mans Will; How *free* foever it be in its acting, yet it has always Good for the object of its choice ; nor can Evil (as fuch) be poffibly defired. Nay, it is Truth of Good, Man properly feeks ; but that Appearances and Colours fhould more often allure us, it is rather the effect of error and weaknefs, than the genuine product of our Wills. As the *Understanding* affects what ought to be *known*, fo the *Will* affects what ought to be *coveted*; only the fenfual part in us over-rules, that ftops the one in its proper purfuit, and fpoils the motion of the other.

We all find in our felves, how earneftly we defire fome *chief Good,* and therefore prefently clofe with Happinefs propofed ; but if this Happinefs be inquir'd into what it is, then indeed we fall off and divide ; which arrifes from the corruptnefs

ruptnefs of mens·affections, that inclining them feveral ways, teach them to fet up feveral Objects, where they wretchedly wander and turn afide, and fo mifs of that which in the general notion they feek after. Yet for all this the Will of Man as it follows Reafon (for fo it differs from *Appetite*) is difpofed by it to follow the beft grounds, and allow particularly of that Good which does moft conduce to its perfection.

And fo I proceed to fhow in the fecond place.

2. The fitnefs of Gods Promifes to inflame Mans Will.

This will appear in that they contain all thofe Topicks of perfwafion that can poffibly belong to any Promife : fuch are *Excellency* of *Good*, *Infallibility of Obtaining*, and a *Miferable defect* as to both thefe in any *other offer* befides.

Now

Now we need not prove in the
Firſt place the *intrinſick Excellency*
of what is *promiſed*, ſince that rich
offer of *Adoption* includes in it what-
ever Gift an All-ſufficient Being
can beſtow. For hereby we are
tranſlated into Gods own Family,
and inveſted with ſuitable Privileges as his Children. All things
are here allowed us that can be
hoped for from a *Father* of *Love*,
·and from a *Lord* of *Power*; which
combining together their *proper
acts*, compleat the Riches of a
Chriſtians Inheritance. In the Old
Teſtament *Father* is not a name
that God was ſtyl'd by, but onely
Lord ; and the Title the Jews had
was that of a *Servant* : which
though it take honour from their
relation to ſuch a Maſter , yet it
imports in it ſelf all the *Burden* of
Duty : But in the New , where
Father and *Lord* are both joyn'd ,
and

and to become *Sons and Daughters,*
is the Privilege of his People;
this speaks at once the *Eafe* of their
Service, and the *Comfort* of their
Hopes as to a *future enjoying.* Indeed God shews in this Covenant
of Grace his utmost contrivance to
draw us to him. As it was the
Confultation of his *Wifdom* at first to
make, so it is here the *labour* of his
Love to *invite* us; for which end
He reveals his Treasures, opens
his Stores, sets out Heaven in its
chief Lights; nay, converts himself
to a Reward. He defired *emptinefs*
to become Man, that He might
take again *fulnefs* to enrich him.
Is it then Life, Joy, Liberty, Glory, or any other Good we count
excellent? Behold! the Purchafe
of it by him who propounds to us
thefe bleffings; and having already *widened* our *Faculties* for *defire,*
He farther *enables* our *Natures* to
receive. Next

Next let us regard the *Infallibility of Obtaining*, which cannot but render a Promise as exceeding worthy to be prized.

The worth and excellency of any Good is a sure foundation of our esteem; but our certainty of having it is that which fixes our Love, and crowns our Endeavours in pursuing it. Now this certainty of ours, as to what God promises, is built upon two great Attributes, *Truth* and *Omnipotence*; which are like Buttresses to support our *Faith* and our *Hope*; the one freeing us from all jealousies of a *deceit*, the other from all dread of a *disappointment*. How can we distrust or fear Gods failing us, that is every way qualified to save! First, the Covenant He makes is fram'd by his *Love*; then *Truth* writes it down; afterwards *Power* comes in

to

to seal up the Assurance ; so that no room is left for any doubt or scruple, since all his Promises are sure ; nor will Mans expectation ever shame him , if *Sin* does not, the onely *blot* of our *hopes* , as well as the *stain* of our *pleasures.* Nothing but Sin can possibly defeat us : it is Sin which undermines all our Blessings, alters our claim and property in Bliss , and gives the *Threatnings* in Scripture Authority to *succeed*. *In him the Promises are Yea and Amen,* that is, firm and stedfast : and when we fall off by a wilfull Apostacy , their *stedfastness* still remains in their own *nature* ; only the benefit of *Application* is lost to Us. But if we once turn to our God by a true Repentance , if we approve our worship of him by the sincerity of our hearts, and the *holiness* of our lives, lo! they are firm and *stedfast faft to us* alfo : God cannot in that cafe exclude us from Heaven; for we bring him the condition of happinefs he requires from us; we produce the *Grace* that leads thither, and know it is impoffible He fhould either deny his own terms, or refufe the likenefs of his Perfections.

The laft thing to be confidered in Gods Promifes, is, That He has provided againft all Temptations from *other offers*, by difperfing a *Vacuum* in things, and leaving nothing here below fit to ftir or move us, except you'l fay *defeĉt of Subftance*, and *want of Certainty* are charms. Were any Good upon Earth adequate to our fouls, had it worth and certainty to attract our defires, then I grant we might juftifie the *byas* of our inclinations that way; becaufe the vifiblenefs of what is offer'd us is a

;farther

farther motive to *turn* them thither; but when *vanity*, nay, *vanity of vanities* is *fuperfcrib'd* upon all the Creation, here is not the leaft colour for our adherence. What is there I pray in this World can be exhibited to us, but fome *Scenes* of Good, and *Images* of an Inheritance? Thus Chrift by the Great *Tempter* was entertained with *Landskips and Shows*, and Kingdoms that were drawn in *Airy Figures*, where the *Delight* could not recompence the *Emptinefs* of the *Profpect*. The like emptinefs is fpread through every thing here; and for any one to reckon upon a fetled Poffeffion, it is like cafting *anchor* upon a *wave*, or binding the *wheels* of *Times motion* : In a word, fuch a Task that has an impoffibility in the Act to baffle the Defign. But where the Promifes are of God there is *weight and ftedfaftnefs* to perfwade us :

weight

weight that can fix all the extra-
vagancy of defire, and ftedfaftnefs
ftrengthen our patience of expect=
ing. Thus you fee the force of the
Motive to confirm that Inference
he makes from it.

I proceed now to handle in the
fecond place.

2. The *Duty* which contains in
it the beft Preparations for receiv-
ing thofe *Promifes* : *Let us cleanfe
our felves from all Filthinefs both of
Flefh and Spirit.*

Where we may take notice,

1. Of the Act, *Cleanfe.*

2. Of the Subject about which
it is employ'd, *Flefh* and *Spirit*,
that is Body and Soul ; fo that a
thorough *Baptifm of the whole man* is
required ; and fuch a wafhing in
the Fountain of Repentance that
purges away inward and outward
defilements.

1. The

1. The Act is remarkable, καθαρίσωμεν, *Let us cleanſe* : a *word* mentioned in the Heathen Schools by way of Speculation, but preſcribed to the Jewiſh and Chriſtian Church as a rule of Practice.

The *Heathens* were not altoge-ther ignorant of it, when they ſtyled *Vertue* it ſelf to be κάθαρσις, a *Cleanſing* ; which the *Platoniſts* give us this account of, namely, That it is a retirement of the Soul within, and a ſeparating from the Body in its motions, when Reaſon acts freely and undiſturbedly, nor has any tincture from the Paſſions to deſile it : ſuch a ſtate ſay they of the Soul is *pure and divine.* This I confeſs may in ſome ſort be call'd a *Purgation*, but it is very defective in another ſenſe, where they ſuppoſe no guilt to be waſhed off, which both Soul and Body have contracted : They regard onely a

E   *refining*

refining of the *Intellectual Powers*, but feek no *purifying* of any *finfull uncleanness.* And this muft be chiefly imputed to that natural *pride* they all had, that they would not allow of a *corrupt fpring*; as we muft owe it wholly to their *ambition*, that they ftudied to advance *Reafon* in its actings; therefore the *Fountain of fin* being unfearch'd, we cannot admit them for Judges here; but ought to confult the *Jewifh* and *Chriftian Church* for the true notion of *Cleanfing.*

In the *Jewifh Church* the outward Ceremony was enjoyn'd, but withal Typical of the *inward*: whence we read in *Exodus* of an exprefs Command before the delivery of the Law, That they fhould *fanctifie themfelves and wafh their cloaths*; from which Precept their Doctors gather that Tenet and Cuftome they had for *Bap-tizing*

tizing all whom they admitted to their *Church and Covenant.*

Now that they fhould thus be *wafh'd* in order to receive the *Law* that was publifhed, it argued both a greatnefs of guilt in the parties, and an abfolute neceffity of repenting, when not fo much as a fpotted Garment was allowed to be near that Mount that quaked and trembled; left the Lightnings of the place fhould break forth to confume, and the Trumpet (there heard) proclaim nothing but Execution. If fuch a preparation were requifite for *hearing* Gods Will, much more was it for *obeying*: whence thofe Sacrifices of old (He commanded) were firft to derive their *cleannefs* from the *Offerer*, and fo had their force of *Legal Attonement.* Were the Offerer not *fanctified* beforehand, all his Worfhip was fpoil'd by reafon of the fpots

E 2 and.

and blemifhes that overfpread it :
The *foulnefs* of his hand laid a *Curfe*
upon the *Expiation*, and by flaying
the *Beaft*, he deftroy'd the *Sacri-*
fice. Therefore a ftrict way of
Cleanfing was obferv'd in the outward man, whereby God led them
to the Spiritual Duty ; as he taught
them by Temporary Promifes to
have a tafte and rellifh of the Heavenly. And left they fhould at any
time forget what was fignified,
their *Purifyings* were *frequently* repeated on them : reprefenting to
them in the fame wafhing *New*
Guilt, and a *New Obligation.*

But the Chriftian Purifying is
of a higher nature , as being *out-*
wardly but *once* ; to fhew *We are bu-*
ried with Chrift by Baptifm into Death,
that like-as He was rais'd from the
Glory of the Father , even fo we alfo
fhould walk in newnefs of Life. Here
is no need of fprinkling Garments,

and Veſſels, nor of ſeparating from the Camp upon an Uncleanneſs, when the whole work of Holineſs is fully exhibited, and one ſolemn Rite introduces the performance.

The work divides it ſelf into two parts, according to the diviſion of mans nature , whereof the firſt is

1. *A cleanſing from the Filthineſs of the Fleſh.*

And good reaſon is there to begin with it : For though *Sin* be properly the *Souls act*, yet by the *Body* it firſt appears ; nay, this Body of ours, being joyned with the Soul , becomes rather a *Miniſter* than an *Inſtrument* in its working ; ſuch a Miniſter that continually provides fewel for the *Hearts luſts*, and makes the corruption of them viſible to the world. If then the *Murdering Sword* be juſtly caſt off, and the *Cup broke* whereby the man

E 3 hath

hath been *poyson'd*, how much more ought this *Principle of Flesh* to be cleansed and subdued, that so deeply shares in the Souls guilt, and proves an *active Executioner* in it ruine! I need not mention the several *works* of it, which the Apostle tells us *are manifest*, because they discover themselves with outward stains and inward impressions upon the consciences of men. Those acts of the *outward man*, that express themselves in worshipping an Idol, in Murder, Sacrilege, Revellings, Lasciviousness and the like, pollute the *Body* that commits them, and convey farther the taint of that pollution to the *Soul*. Nor can Men with all their art so colour and disgrace what is convey'd there, as that the nature of its deformity should be changed; but the *Corruptions of Flesh* will still abide *frightful* even in the midst of

their

their *Conqueft.* Sin then carrying its own Conviction, the great Query is, How we fhould purge it? But to this the Affiftance of Grace, and Mans Refolution is re= quired : the former will not fail if the latter be prefent ; nor will the latter be wanting if Gods *Pro- mifes* be the *Object.* Where *thefe* are ftedfaftly beheld , they will furely melt and diffolve us, power= fully break our rocky hearts, and engage us anew in a Life of Ho- linefs.

Goodnefs is commanding in its own nature, and *enthrones* it felf in Mans Will; nor needs it other force for keeping its *Soveraignty*, but what it continually carries by *charming* the *affections.* And this Goodnefs is fully feen in Gods *Pro= mifes* : all the *Vail* is taken off, which is generally caft upon Pro- vidence ; and inftead of glimpfes

and

and *half-lights* we are allowed a
full diſcovery of their glory ; ſuch
a one in its working that can
joyn *ſurprize*, *delight* and *victory* together. For all the Graces of a Saviour are here ſhown , and al the
Riches of Eternity are here manifeſted ; which muſt needs take a-
way the reſiſtance of *Fleſh*, provided we be fixt in our Contempla-
tions.

Why then are we not ſerious in
weighing theſe things ? why does
not Love, nor Mercy conſtrain us ?
I am ſure no carnal Temptation
can be endued with ſuch ſtrength :
It is ſeated in *Fleſh*, which is *weakneſs*, and only conquers that Heart
which is unprepar'd.   The Queſtion that was put to *Pyrrhus* when
he had in his head the deſign of
conquering many Kingdoms, may
be put to the purſuers of Sin in
thoſe various *forms* and *faſhions of*
                              Appetite,

Appetite, what it is they intend by all the Travel they make through a World of Corruption. Perhaps they will fay (as he did, when we have compaffed our defigns we will thenbe quiet, and live to our felves : but to this the reply is ftrong and forcible; why will they not be quiet now, and live to themfelves in a fervice of their God, when that knowledge of e-vil they feek after is purchafed with trouble, and manifeft dan-ger of their Souls? Therefore whe-ther we would confult our own Intereft, or witnefs our Gratitude to God for his Promifes, we are bound to be refolute and fpeedy in the *cleanfing* of this *Flefh*, which at the beft is but a *burden*, and fin gives it a farther *weight* to crufh and deftroy us.

But that we may perform this *Duty* aright, Two Rules are to be
ob-

observed by us, which are here intimated in my Text.

1. That the Object of our
cleansing be *all Filthiness of the
Flesh.*

2. That the work which refers
to it, be so effectual, as that no
Filthiness should return.

The first of these is necessary,
because indeed without it there is
no *cleansing* ; for wherever Filthiness is but in *part* washed off, the
whole is still denominated impure.
Who will call that Body sound,
where the disease shifts places, but
is not altogether removed ? No
more can we call that *Flesh cleans'd,*
where Vice changes its seat, but
never loses its commanding power. It is true an Hypocrite may
look fair in the worlds eye after a
superficial purging of some corruption ; but that cheat he puts
upon others alters not the uncleanness

nefs of his own temper. The Character of things remain fixt how
changeable foever be mens Judgments. It is faid of *Myriam* the *Le-
per*, that fhe appeared *white as
fnow* ; but none could conclude
from that *whitenefs* any thing, except the malignancy of her *difeafe* ;
where the *mafs* of *blood* being taint-
ed,the Body became wan and pale
like a *Dead Carcafe.* Such is the
whitenefs of fome Profeffors in thofe
half-acts of outward Purity ; It is
but a *Leprous Hypocrifie,* which argues *deadnefs* and *rottennefs* within.
But in Gods and Scripture account
none are truly *clean* in the outward
man, but thofe that purge out every thing which defiles it : in whom
the *health* and *complexion* is found by
a *vigorous* expelling of all corruption. In thefe the Spirit truly
worketh ; and they fhow their
fanctifying *Principle* to rule in them
by.

by an univerfal effect that follows
it : For thus Gods Spirit acts in Believers, diffufing its vertue through
all parts, nor can any deed pafs it
uncleanfed : But when men folely
act by their own fpirit (which has
a partial influence) then they fin-
gle out fome *enormous Vice*, fome
provoking Goliah to kill ; which
were a happy Conqueft, did it
make an impreffion upon the grofs
of an *Army* ; but alas ! here execution is done, and not at all followed with any weakning in the
Body.

Again, the fecond is neceffary,
becaufe a *Relapfe* into *Filth* fpoils
the fruit of the former *cleanfing*,
and withal doubles the *ftain.*
Therefore to prevent a guilt of
that kind in this *Body of flefh*, it
muft be our *continued work* to fub-
due it : The only way to affure us
of *Sins Death*, is by perfevering to
deftroy

deftroy its Dominion : that *Samp-*
fon within muft be continually
fhav'd; nay the razor muft pierce
deep to the very *roots*, otherwife
his *ftrength is not gone.* Little feve-
rities upon a remorfe are no better than a Drunkards fobernefs in
his *qualms* ; which he then *dies to,*
but not to his *fin* : fhort penances
upon check are but an Adulterers
Whip , whereby he lets out *Blood*
to cool a prefent *Burning*, but not
to end the *Difeafe.* O the Art of a
Profeffor in thus fubduing his carnal motions ; when he choofes for
a while the method of Rigour,
only to give him eafe in new fins!
Many can turn *Hermits* that way;
with whom a fufpence of their luft
is but a preparative to frefh vi-
gour : they endure much to fin
more ; and make ufe of hardfhip
to become helpful to their corruptions, as Frofts and Snows are

to

to Seed, which they seem to lock up and bury in the ground, but indeed improve it for multiplying. If this be a *cleansing from all filthiness of the flesh,* then let them that study an increase of their lust be styl'd the only Champions to overcome it. But wouldst thou have the true glory of it? then deny thy self constantly in a Temptation, and hold out to the last in the discipline of Repentance: So this Body of Sin will appear utterly defeated when thou bringest Time as a witness of thy *Victory.*

But there remains in the second place another sort of *cleansing.*

2: *From all filthiness of the Spirit.* This is not so much considered in the world; but surely there is in some respects more of sin, and consequently more of defilement than in Carnal corruption. Such are those inward spots, of Pride, Malice,

lice, Envy, Hypocrifie, Diftruft of God ; to conclude, all thofe finful motions which it is proper for *Spirits* to be guilty of.

The Enormity of them will appear upon Three accounts.

1. In that they are the *fpring* of all *outward filthinefs*. For from the *Heart* it is (or the *fpiritual part* in man) that Fornication, Drunkennefs and Blafphemy flow ; whence if thefe and the like fins have all the foulnefs of tincture on them, the *Sink* whence they iffue muft be much more defil'd. Were evil Thoughts effectually reftrain'd in us, all the ftream of carnal wickednefs would be cut off; which made *Solomon* call for our greateft care over the Heart, where finful Imaginations are cherifhed. *Keep thy heart* (fays he) *with all diligence ; for out of it are the Iffues of Life* ; ay and of *Death too* when it is not rightly

rightly govern'd in its motions. An evil Heart makes an adulterous Eye, a deceitful Tongue, a violent Hand : All outward crimes are the Offspring of the Thoughts; therefore *these* (being the *Parent-sins*) are the more aggravated in their guilt, as the *cause* of *others.*

2. In that they are *purely* the *Souls work*, and that in its *strength*, without the dregs of matter, or the weakness of flesh to interpose.

What *Jacob* said to *Reuben, Thou art my First-born , my might, and the beginning of my strength, the excellency of dignity, and the excellency of power,* the same may be applied to those actions which *primarily* issue from the *Soul.* And so when they prove sinful, they derive from the *Dignity* of those noble faculties the greater *shame.* It is the Devils way thus to offend ; and howsoever he may

tempt

tempt us to *deeds of Flesh*, yet he is
as to himself only an Agent in such
sins that pollute the *mind*, and defile the *conscience*, so that he is a
Rebel in all the height and excellency of Being, and knowing no
Body to defile him, as an *Unclean*
Spirit, he dishonours his nature,
and against the *God of Spirits* does
immediately make war. So then
when our hearts are alike stain'd,
when our *Filthiness* becomes spiritual, we then bear his Image in the
true Character. Now what can be
greater disgrace to our Natures
than this is? For the highest Perfection we can ever arrive to is to
be *like God*; and that is to resemble him in *Holiness*, which chiefly
consists in the *purity of our minds*;
On the other side the greatest *Fall*
we can be ever condemn'd to, is to
be *like Satan*, and that is to resemble him in *Uncleanness*, which chief=

F   ly

ly confifts in the *foulnefs* of our *Souls* ; whence thefe Souls of ours muft needs contract a great guilt, when bad thoughts do defile them; wherein we carry the very picture of the Father, and bear his ftamp in the crime.

3. As they are the *work*, fo they are the full *delight.* of the Inward man. Here the Soul *centers* within it felf, and uncontrollably embraces its own actings ; and the fecretnefs of thofe ftains renders them difficult to be cleanfed; whereas thefe *flefhly motions* cannot breed any fulnefs of pleafure; and their pollutions being evident, do often check the committer with thofe Three reftraints to a Rational Being, which are *Law*, *Confcience* , and *Fame*. And therefore changes are many times wrought in the greateft Sinners ; but when Sin once retires to *Invifible Garri-*

sons, it is seldom deftroy'd, becaufe neither Law nor Fame have here place, and Confcience is too weak to overcome. Upon this account the labour of cleanfing is here ne-ceffary, and the Soul muft be brought to encounter it felf in all the *fubtilty of a reforming,* that we may prefent to our God in Pure Flefh a mortified Spirit.

Now fhould Uncleannefs be in-wardly cherifhed, what-ever the outward acts of fanctity be, they are to be reckoned no better than *Pilate's* purifying before the Mul-titude, when he wafht his hands, but fuffered the guilt of the moft innocent *Blood* to pafs uncleanfed. Yet how many are there that reft in a Shape and Outfide of Piety! a Privilege (if they will call it one) which the *Old Serpent* can challenge; who in the midft of his Curfe does yet *gild* his *Spots* with

fair

f air Light, and in a *form* of *Bleffed=*
nefs lays his *Sting.* But a *Bodily*
purging (take it at the beft) is only
the *Preface* to a new Life: an intro-
ductory part to true Holinefs : It
is a Dedication of the *Court* to pre=
pare the Offering upon the *Altar*;
and 'tis the Altar you know fancti-
fies the Gift; fo 'tis the Heart that
qualifies the performance. If we
go no higher than *bare Flefh,* we are
but like the *Bullocks* that were
cleanfed; but if befides that Purifying we are fpiritually Holy, we
become like the *Prieft* that *facri-*
ficed.

Now to attain fuch a ftate as
that is, a watchful jealoufie is requifite over our Souls : and here,
as we muft doubtfully *fufpect,* fo
we ought immediately to *fupprefs*
any fpringing Temptation. It is
eafie to caft out the Adverfary
while he is weak; fuch are all
Filthy

Filthy Thoughts in their *Infancy*; but let them once spread and grow in the mind, then it is difficult for any one to check and subdue them. Who knows not what eafinefs there is in quenching a *spark*, or turning as one pleafes a *little current*? But if the Spark gets fewel to feed on, and enlarges it felf into a great Flame, how often does it mock mens labour and pains to hinder the mifchief of its progrefs? So likewife a little current, if it be fupplyed from Floods, and allowed to fwell with frefh ftreams, how ungovernable is its courfe! After the fame manner do *Spiritual Luftings* prove furious and wild, when they get their fewel and fupply from the will and affections flowing in. It is very needful then for thee to guard thy *Heart*, which is fo apt to breed fin, and fo ready to ftrengthen an

F 3 evil

evil purpofe. But for the better
fecuring of it, oh labour ftedfaftly
to apprehend thy God, not only
as the accurate *Beholder*, but as the
fevere *Judge* and *Punifher* of the
Inner man. Indeed God does not
exercife fuch a Vifible Judgment
upon any *fpiritual filthinefs* in this
World, becaufe He is mainly con-
cern'd here (*as a Governour*) to prevent the mifchiefs of *outward actions*, for the better defence of humane Fellowfhip; but when all
worldly Societies fhall ceafe, and
every one be fummoned to his
Tribunal, He will then proceed *as
a Lawgiver*, demanding a ftrict account according to the full extent
and compafs of his Laws; and fo
thefe *Spiritual Sins* will be vifibly
punifhed, in that they are fuch e-
vident breaches of his Spiritual
Commands. It is my duty then
chiefly to prepare for that Day ;
nor

nor am I fo much to examin the manner of his Government in this life, as how He will deal with me in another : Since that is the proper ftate, wherein I fhall be ever fixt and determined, and wherein his Juftice (that fummons me) will be clearly revealed. Thus fhould every one employ his Meditations , and whoever bufies himfelf in them, he will find this to be the fruit and fuccefs of them, that he will thereby get armour of defence within, and difcourage the *Tempter* from affaulting.

Thus much for the *Duty*.

The Third Particular I am to handle is

3. The Manner of performing the Duty enjoyn'd us ; namely a *Perfecting of Holinefs in Gods Fear* : where we may note Two things.

1. The Degree or Meafure we fhould contend after, namely *Perfection.* F 4 2. The

2. The Inward Principle that ought to quicken us, a *Godly Fear.*

The former shows we need a continual Progress in a Religious course ; the latter shows we need a faithful direction to a right object.

1. For the *Degree* or *Measure* we should contend after, this imports no less than a summoning of all the Powers of the Soul, and the setting of a Task to our outward members, that both in Mind and Body we may render to our God an unspotted Sacrifice. Such an Offering (as this is) is not in an *instant* to be performed; nor does God so fit any Saint, as that his Initials should be full. His *Justification* of a Sinner may be compleat *in one act*, when he gives him a *Legal discharge* ; but his *Sanctifying* of us is not thus *perfected* ; because it is such a work of his Spirit in us, that

that *gradually* proceeds to the expelling of Sin, and takes in our
Endeavours to *grow up* and *encreafe*
in holy duties. There is fiift an
Infancy in the new nature, where
(all the parts being form'd) *Inno-*
cence is written as a *Charatter to be*
kept, but not its *Weaknefs* : for a
farther advancement is ftill look'd
for ; whence the ftrength of Men
and perfectnefs of Stature is required in a Chriftian.

Truly how can we imagine beginnings fhould fuffice, or that we
fafely can reft in them, when the
remainders of concupifcence within, the temptations without to
which we are fubject, the proper
fruits and effects of a Faith juftifying, laftly, the neceffity of imita-
ting our Divine Pattern, do all call
for labour, ftrife and diligence in
our Chriftian race, that we fall
not fhort of Heaven by but a little
entring

entring the way thither? *Naaman's* wafhing in *Jordan feven times*, as it reprefented to him the Greatnefs of his Leprofie, fo it reprefents to us thofe *repeated acts* God expects from us of a naked fearch into our ways, and that accompanied with a frequent purging of all the filth we contracted. Here is an evidence of Gods *adopting* us that we do ἐπιτελεῖν ἁγιατύνην, that is, *finifh and bring to end the work of Holinefs* : otherwife we are as unfafe in our *cleanfing*, as thofe *Swine* were which the Devil hurried into the *Sea*, making their firft *cleannefs* and their laft deftruction to go together.

But we muft obferve in the fecond place,

2. *The Principle* that ought to quicken us, *a Godly Fear*; and this is the Point I fhall conclude with.

But fome may ask why is *Fear* brought in when Gods *Promifes* are

the

the motive? Is not *Love* the natural confequent of fuch offers, and
a Principle too of it felf more
binding?

I anfwer, *Love* is not the fole
confequent, but *Fear* alfo, by rea=
fon of thofe conditions upon which
the Promifes hang; and this Fear
of the Two is more binding; as
urging upon us a fenfe of danger,
and thereby quickning us unto a-
ction; whereas Love without is
faint, and altogether languifhes in
its working.

Now this Principle of *Godly Fear*
excludes utterly the Heathens way
of purifying, as a *Rite* in its ufing
unclean: For fo every thing becomes
to an Unbeliever: It excludes likewife thofe feeming religious acts
of Pretending Chriftians, who
in the good things they do, have
either a *dread* of *Punifhment*, or the
vanity of *Opinion* for their Object.
The

The one confifts not with this in my Text, which purely terminates in God alone, and the other deftroys all the notion of a true Worfhip, when it fets up an Idol of Applaufe.

Yet thus do Hypocrites boaft of Holinefs; to fome parts of which perhaps Legal Terrors, or the regard of Men may conftrain them; nothing is natural in their Religion but forc'd; and the *fpring* of their *motion* is without them; fo that they are rather to be counted *artificial Engines* (produced to caft forth water upon an *open burning*) than *Chriftians* that are free and active at all *times* to extinguifh the Flame. But if fuch as thefe be excluded, how much more the loofely prophane! who cannot be thought to have a touch of this Paffion when they defy God and his Laws. Did a *right fear* once rule

rule and fway the Confcience, it were neither poffible for vice to be barefac'd, nor for Hypocrifie to be difguifed : The awe of a God would *fhame* the one, and *ftrip* the other of its *Covering.* But behold ! the mafque, the difguife is not fo much the danger of this Age ; we are fallen from *fhows* to a *contempt* of Chriftianity, from *colours* to *open war* : our *paint* is turn'd to *rottennefs* ; and the *perfume* of our Profeffion is become like the *air of fnuffs* , nay the noifome *fmell* of corrupted Bodies, that can *kill* at a *diftance*, and by their power of Execution fadly manifeft Death has not deftroy'd them. O the extremes of Sin ! whither is the triumph & glory of our Religion departed ! Is it not now a matter of boafting to *kick* at *Heaven*, while the *head* at the fame time knocks the *Earth*, and calls for the opening of a *Grave* ? Is it not the

triumph

triumph of *wit* to fport at a *Luft*, when it reproaches the Committer in the act, and tells him farther by its *fting* that his own *fcoffs* are *re-veng'd*? But what is it we truft to in this our offending? God we know is above, has a hand of Juftice to ftrike, nor can any promife tye it up, when once forfeited by our tranfgreffions. All our fhift for finning is to hinder Confcience from interpofing, by cutting off all ferioufnefs of thought, and defperately throwing onr felves into a *Gulf* of pleafure. In the mean time, while we are funk in ways of iniquity, Judgment is ripening over us; clouds gather about us thicker and blacker, and the lightning of Gods wrath is fitted and prepared; nor can we efcape the force of it, except we remove the Seeds of our ruine by a fpeedy and univerfal repentance.

The

The *Spartans* we read were great *Worshippers* of the *Passions* ; and therefore had *Temples* erected to them ; but *Fear* was the *Goddess* they chiefly *worshipped* in regard of its use and influence to preserve States. Certainly though they erred in thus dedicating their Temples, yet they did not erre in their notion of the advantage of *Fear* : but had a *godly one* fully possessed them , they would much more have concluded the safety of a Nation to depend on it ; as being the surest Bond of Law, and the only preventer of Gods Plagues. I need not endeavour to prove either of these ; for where such a *Fear* has due place, it will in the closest *secresie* oblige men to *obey*, and engage God *openly* to *defend* them. But whether outward prosperity be always the fruit, I shall not enquire : I am sure the success

is

is of the laft day, and the fentence of mercy waits onely upon thofe that religioufly *fear* to offend. To thefe no death can be fudden nor untimely , which alone is the portion of impenitent finners; who fall often to the earth with their *Youth* and with their *Sins* too as *full blown* : and being caft down by a Judgment, are not allowed a fpace to recover them. Why then will we abufe the promifes that are offer'd us? There is a *Golden thread* of them let down from Heaven, but tyed to a *Sword* with the *point* over us; and while we are rioting and in-dulging the Flefh, the thread is ready to break, and the Sword to fall on us.

Pardon the harfhnefs of de-nouncing thefe things; for foft words are not for Minifters to de-liver : It is your confcience we are

bound

bound to ftrike, whereas your eyes are enough enlightned. And the Corruption of mens natures requires this Method, that *Promifes* and *Threatnings* fhould be joyn'd, to chaftife and temper our hopes, and fettle upon our fpirits a right frame. Otherwife we fhould boldly prefume, and learn no *Holinefs in Gods Fear*, but that Good and Evil poffeffing our thoughts, help to quicken us in our Obedience.

So then I befeech you contemplate Divine Love, as withal fatal to the refufer : joyn the *Father* with the *Judge*, and the *Adoption* he offers with his *Severity* in *condemning* : farther confider how the *Dignity* of *Humane Nature* lies in the *purenefs of its faculties*, as a *Reward* follows their *Exercife* : Firft you are advanced by it to be like God, next in that likenefs to enjoy him : Laft of all, fearch out every motive

G   tive

tive to prefs you to. Holinefs, which if you enter upon and perfevere in, the fame God (who was Gracious in making, and is Faithful in performing what He has promifed) will enftate you in the Inheritance of Sons, and add Eternity for its Crown.

The

The Third Difcourfe.

St. John 6. 68.

Then Simon Peter anfwered him, Lord to whom ſhall we goe ? Thou haſt the words of Eternal Life.

IF you examin the fcope of thefe words, they are a full and paffionate reply to that Queſtion Chriſt made in the verfe foregoing, where He tries the Faith of his Apoftles, whether they would conftantly adhere to his Laws, or with the reſt of the Multitude forfake him? For we read in this Chapter how that great Crowd of people which followed him, began now to fhrink and fall off, becaufe his *Doctrine* was (like his *Perfon*)

no wayes fuited to a carnal Ap-
prehenfion. And the colour they
had for this their *Apoftacy* was fome
fuppofed abfurdity of what he taught;
as when He ftyl'd himfelf *the Li-*
Verf. 51. *ving Bread which came down from*
Heaven, *and whoever eat of that*
Bread fhould live for ever : So that
we find upon an enquiry that a
bare *Metaphor* was the quarrel, and
a *Figure of Speech* the foundation of
the Controverfie.

But waving the fubject matter
of their Difpute (which is at large
defcribed in the Chapter) it will
not be impertinent to obferve the
ftrange levity and ingratitude of
the Vulgar, who being the worft
judges of a difcourfe, will yet prefume to fit upon it ; and if it once
croffes their fancy, they are ready
to throw off the Authority of
their Lord ; ay and fuch an Authority, that was before highly
com-

commended to them in all the Wonders of Mercy. Hence it is said (*v. 66.*) *That many of his Disciples went back, and walked no more with him.*

Upon so general a *revolt* He appears at that accident unconcern'd : whatever pitty He had for their persons, yet He leavs them to be punished by that *flight* they had made ; but as for the *Twelve* (whom He had particularly chosen for his Attendants) these He deals with as a Friend , founds their Loyalty, and by his very seeming to doubt of it, shows all the Tenderness of a Saviour. *Then said He to the Twelve, Will ye also go away? Then Simon Peter answered him, Lord , to whom shall we go? Thou hast the words of Eternal Life.*

In this Answer of *St. Peters* we may consider Two Particulars.

1. The Sense of all the Apostles

deli-

delivered by one of them, which was plainly this, That they ought not to feek another Mafter.

2. The Reafon of their Choice drawn from the fingular excellency of his *Teaching*, *Thou haft the words of Eternal Life.*----

I begin with their General Senfe, *Lord to whom fhall we go?* which kind of fpeech does imply, that fhould they offer to leave Chrift, yet a Mafter was needful to be their Guide in Religion. For fuch is mans weaknefs and poverty by nature, that he requires fomewhat without him to reft on for Happinefs: but it here farther fignifies, that they were already fixt upon a Teacher, and could find out nothing comparable to him they heard. This is the fcope and meaning of the Queftion.

From the *Matter* thus declared, and from the *Occafion* of doing it,

we

we may note Two things.

1. The Noblenenefs of a right Faith when once feated in the Soul.

2. The Authority of Truth notwithftanding the Oppofition of the World.

1. The *Noblenefs of a right Faith*, &c.---- And it is this, That it fets upon Difficulties and conquers them : Let the times of Profeffion be bad and reproachful too for thofe numbers that backflide, yet he that is well grounded in his Belief, has his thoughts higher planted. He is above the Poor Circumftance of time , and beyond the Contagion of an Example. Now the rules that govern moft men in their courfe are Private Intereft and Publick Opinion; fo that like *Puppits* they move, and the principle of their acting is without them ; but he that is led by nei-

ther

ther of thefe, but makes *Religion*
his *Intereſt*, and obedience to it his
Fame, he may be call'd a Believer
indeed : for he exprefles the Man
and the Chriſtian together. Others
are but *Reeds* in their Station, ſha-
ken with every *wind*, and mark'd
for their *barrenneſs* while they ſtand;
but he is a *Tree* fet by the *Rivers
of water*, that has *depth* of root and
fruitfulneſs to crown it. Yet the
conſtancy he has is not any ſtiffneſs of mind , that proceeds from
the prejudice of Education; for
that is no better than the *ſtiffneſs
of earth*, which is fenſeleſs in that
condition ; but it is a vigorous
judgment ſways him to the act,
and confirms his faculties in working.

I grant it very difficult at firſt
to *believe*, becauſe of the *Enmity of
Fleſh*, and the *Sophiſtry of Reaſon* ,
which is *Fleſh* fet out in another figure ;

gure ; but where *Faith* gets an entrance, there flesh is subdued and reason answer'd,& the heart comes prepared to embrace Christianity in its hardeft terms. For this is a Principle that humbles and lays us low, and difcovers our weaknefs to our felves : It forces us to confefs that God has *depths* of his own we cannot fathom; and fince we allow our affent to *Myſteries* in Nature, no lefs ought we to do fo to *Myſteries* in *Religion*, though not to be explain'd by our narrow underſtanding. This was the Apoſtles cafe, who learnt to fubmit to the Doctrine that was preach'd, and deriv'd from that fubmiffion a courage to adhere. Let us confider next

2. *The Authority of Truth notwithſtanding the Oppoſition of the World.*

God never left himfelf without witnefs in the midſt of the greateſt Apoſtacies.

Apoſtacies. He had *Noah* to be his Champion in the *Old World*, *Elijah* in *Iſrael*, and Apoſtles in the *Infancy* of the *Chriſtian Church*, that kept up Religion from periſhing. *Truth* and *Light* have this property common to them both, that as they are apt to be clouded, ſo they have vertue to break through thoſe Miſts that interpoſe. There is a natural Soveraignty in them both, and they ſeem to be born to an Univerſal Inheritance : though they may be as Strangers and Exiles in ſome lands, yet in others they take the Poſſeſſion.

We all know the force of a *good title*, how it prevails. If a *Prince* of undoubted right be caſt off by the vile treachery of his own Subjects, yet his *Title* will ſtill rule; powerfully poſſeſſing the peoples hearts, and as ſtrongly *warring* in the *conſcience* of an *Uſurper.* The
like

like command has the Caufe of
Truth amongft Men, and a furer
too; for a People may be fcourg'd
by a total lofs of their Prince; but
Gods Faithfulnefs is ingag'd to
maintain the Dominion of the o-
ther. He that created and eftablifhed all things by the *word of*
his power, has fpoken this, that
Truth fhall for ever endure; and
in order to accomplifh what He
has fpoken, he employs his *Spirit*
to work; gives us natures inqui-
fitive and reflecting, whereby we
are ftirred up to the duties of Piety; fo that as long as the *Spirit* a-
bides (which is *eternal*) as long as
Reafon and *Confcience* laft (which
are *effential* to our *frame*) the Characters of Religion muft for ever
remain. Whether it be of the Ef-
fence of Gods *Church* to be always
vifible, I fhall not difcufs; but the
foundation upon which it is built,

can

can certainly never fail, since He is God that is laid there. *For other Foundation can no man lay, than that is laid, which is Jesus Christ.*

Should we now on the other side consider the growth of *Error,* and the fair show it makes in the world, we cannot conclude hence that it has strength to continue. For strength presuppofes a real exi-stence in the Subject; whereas *Er=ror* is of it self a *meer nothing,* and ows to *Ignorance* that it appears. It is a *Ghost* that walks in the *dark,* whose *body* is fram'd by our *fancies,* and when *day* comes, it *vanishes* with them. But to *Truth* a *being* pertains, and it constantly strives to open its way into *Light,* to re-veal that Being to others, which when effected, it gloriously spreads, and enlarges its *Empire* with that discovery.

Before

Before I pass to the second Head
of my Discourse, I shall briefly
dispatch one Quere, which is this:
Why *Simon Peter* (that singly spoke
here) should so readily proclaim
his own Faith, and undertake likewise for the Faith of the *Apostles*,
though a *Judas* was of their number.

Now the reason of this I can
only resolve into those Two Graces, wherein he excell'd *Zeal* and
Charity. The one made him for-
ward in a publick *Confession* of him-
self, the other in a *Defence* of his
Brethren. Zeal is a fire that will
be sure to get uppermost; whence
our *Apostle* being heated with it,
comes out first for his *Lord*; but
then left the ambition of that act
should urge him to pursue his own
Glory, he religiously suppresses it
by his Charity to others. It is the
nature of Charity to be kind, and
free

free from envy; not to seek her
own but anothers praise : It treats
all persons alike, except some vi-
sible fruits do distinguish them ;
and brings a Garment along with
it of an equal breadth to hide every right Professor ; in a word, it is
a generous Vertue, enobling our
works of piety, and making us be-
neficial to the world.

This was the temper of our
blessed *Apostle*, whom many are
prone enough to imitate for his
Zeal; but if this latter Grace be
wanting, they ought to suspect
the birth of that *flame*; since the
true *Gospel-fire* that comes down
from *Heaven* has a comforting
warmth in it that *heals*, and tends
not to kill, but to *save*.

I come now to my Second Head,
where we have

2. The reason of their choice
drawn from the singular Excellency

lency of Chrifts Teaching.--- *Thou haft the words of Eternal Life.*

It might be expected that *poor Fifhermen* (as thefe were) fhould have had *Souls* as *low* as their *Trade* : that they fhould be far from conceiving, and farther yet from purfuing a ftate of eternity ; whofe great end and bufinefs before was but the *fmall gain* of a *draught* ; neither knew they how to prize any greater wealth, than what a *Lake* or a *Brook* contains. But fee how Religion exalts them; what high thoughts are now form'd, and what vaft defires are rais'd in them by the force of their Mafters Difcipline ; fo that they begin to defpife a prefent Good, and breath after nothing but a future Reward. Temporal Dominion was below their aim ; for who can imagine they fhould propound to themfelves an *Earthly Monarchy*, that

stuck

ftuck only to Chrift for an *Invifible Crown?* Truly the manner of his *appearance* in this our Flefh, and the nature of his *Doctrine* taught them no other : His appearance was fo mean that it was but the *form of a Servant* which He affum'd ; Agen, his Doctrine was fo *fpiritual*, that Joh.17.36, He challeng'd only a *Kingdom di-*
Luke 9. 2. *ftinct* from the *World*, and fent only his Difciples upon that Errand to *preach* it.

But the *Pretended Succeffors* of *St. Peter* (who here follows his Lord for his *Heavenly Miniftry*) can arrogantly purfue a *worldly claim* ; as if *Earth* were in their *Charter* as well as *Heaven*, and therefore they ought to take both by *violence*, pull down Kings and Princes, and advance themfelves to an arbitrary Greatnefs. Whofe *Apoftles* I pray are they that would thus rule ? or by what right of donation do the King-

Kingdoms of the world belong to them? For we do not read they were any of thofe *Gifts Chrift gave* 4 Mat. 8. *unto men*, but onely the *Devils offer*, which He rejected. I am fure fuch as thefe are the Greateft Perfecu= tors of our Lord. The putting of a *Reed* into his hand before he fhould *fuffer*, was but the *mocking* of his *Power* ; but to put a *Sword* into his hand that is come to *fave* us, is a flat denyal of his *Goodnefs*, and fo they impioufly number him with the *Tranfgreffors*. I need not farther enlarge on this Subject, nor demonftrate the wildnefs of their Tenet, which both our Sa- viours Life, and manner of Go- vernment, the Commands and Practife of the Apoftles, the Ex- amples of primitive Martyrs, and in a word, the Profeffion of the beft Saints has condemn'd. But this by the way----It here lies upon me to prove how Chrifts *words* are the *proper words* of *Eternal Life* ; which may be eafily made out from that Gofpel he has deliver'd to his Church; wherein we find him.

1. *A Minifter* , in that He has fully reveal'd it to the World.

2. *A Purchafer* , in that he has acquired a right to beftow it.

3. *A Worker* , in that He has made the Doctrine of it effectual to Salvation.

I. *A Minifter* , *in that he has fully reveal'd it to the World* , as He did alfo the Doctrine of *Eternal Death* , which I before handled. And He has revealed *this Life* in a way of Authority and Sweetnefs proper to himfelf, at once forcing us to affent to the truth of that evidence, and raifing our affections to purfue it. He therefore delivered it in fuch a Style that might power-

fully

fully engage us both ways : as when He did not onely exprefly mention the thing it felf, but likewife defcribed it by fuch inviting Charaders, as *Joy*, *Glory*, *the King-dom of Heaven*; nay, in a peculiar Emphafis, *the Kingdom* where Life and Immortality are *enthron'd.*

Now who is there but muft acknowledge the blindnefs that cover'd the *Gentile World*, till this Great Prophet came to enlighten us ? For we fat in darknefs, and in the very fhadow of Death, which encompaffed us round and befet us, and took away from us any farther Profpect; not to be open'd nor enlarg'd, till this Light came, which *gave us Knowledg and Salva-tion.* What force foever there may be in *Natural Religion* (which fome boaft of) yet the great Mafters of thofe Schools which taught it, were miferably dimfighted as to

H 2   any

any future state of Life and Happiness, except wee'l say a walk
in *Elysium* for *Wandring Souls*, or a
wretched *Pilgrimage* through *seve=
ral Bodies*, be a proper Condition
to be desired. Yet thus did the
best of those Writers dream, who
apprehended well enough a God
and his Worship; and though they
might deliver fine notions of both,
yet *fancy* came in to corrupt all
with gross devices and foolish mix=
tures in their Reward. Hence the
morality even of their Chiefest was
suited to their Principles; that is,
They had the *Shadow* of a *Good Life*,
as they had the *Shadow of Immortality*. The greatest height of vertue they ever arriv'd to, was but
to disguise their Passions, and by
stopping some foul effects of them
to consult a Fame of well-doing,
whereas the seed and root of a
corruption was still cherished, and
lust

luft fecretly ruled in their hearts and lives, for want of a difcovery which we Chriftians enjoy about the eternal Wages of our deeds. Upon this account *Tertullian* and the reft of the Ancients had fufficient ground to condemn their choiceft *Philofophy*, fince the ftudy of it was followed with no other fruit than this, That it ferv'd for *Paint* to hide Vice, but prov'd no *Antidote* to expell it.

But if *Natural Reafon* did thus fail, muft we alfo complain of any defect in thofe *Infpirations* which Gods own *Prophets* were affifted with? No; for the words they delivered were *words of life* : onely the *Jews* that heard them were in their nonage, bred up at firft with *milk and honey*, and that *Infant-food of a Carnal Promife* : and therefore it was judg'd fit by Divine Wifdom to wean them by degrees

H 3 from

from thefe outward things, and not allow them a *Spiritual Diet* of per= fect *happinefs*, till they arrived at the ftrength of a Mafculine Under= ftanding. But the Prophets them= felves had that ftate revealed to them in all its clearnefs ; only that *Difcipline*, which their Hearers were under, cauf'd it to be difpenc'd to them by a *Figurative application*.

But Chrift came in the very fulnefs of time, when *Life and Im= mortality* were to be fhown ; and He anfwer'd that fulnefs by his own Teaching : fo that all thofe Prophets who went before him, ferv'd but like the light of a *Morn- ing-ftar* to ufher in the brightnefs of that difcovery. Let us confider him in the next place.

II. As a *Purchafer*, in that *He acquir'd a right to beftow it*. And this Title He has to fuch a donation by that Price he laid down for his

own

own People, when He bought them out of their old Thraldom, and cancell'd that forfeiture they had made of *Life Eternal*, by the merits of his Death, and the infinite Satisfaction of his Sufferings. His Gofpel is the Evidence of this his Purchafe, wherein *Eternal Life* and our Lords *Propriety* is declard; whereby He is qualified not only to poffefs it *in himfelf*, but to conferre that Inheritance upon *others.* And therefore to him we muft have recourfe in all our Devotions, and upon his *Merits alone* ground our addreffes, *who is able to fave to the uttermoft them that come unto God by him.* Heb. 7. 25.

But the *Romanifts* feem to have found out other Purchafers, at leaft many Sharers with him in that Prerogative; when dividing the Vertue of his Mediation, they fly to *Saints and Angels* by a *folemn in-*

H 4. *vocation*

vocation of them to intercede. What is this elfe but an *Idolatrous act*, when the *Creature* is fet up by them for a peculiar *Object* they muft *adore*, and for a *Meritorious Helper they should truft to?* or where= in do they differ from the old *Heathens*, who worfhipped their *Demons* or Inferiour Gods as *intermediate Agents* with the *Supreme?* If they upon that fcore were condemned as *Idolaters* by the ancient maintainers of our Religion, certainly a like charge does moft defervedly fall upon fuch Worfhippers that parcel out and communicate *Divine Glory*; nay, the Charge is much heavier in this refpect, becaufe the Heathens were ignorant of Gods will; but for Chriftians this way to *beg life*, it is to libel Gods Word that fpeaks otherwife; it is to exclude his Son from his own Office and Royalty, in whofe *Name* we are bid *to pray*, and by whom *alone* we have accefs to our Heavenly Father; nay it is repugnant to the condition of thofe *Spirits* above, who can neither hear every mans prayers throughout the world , nor look into the hearts of thofe that call on them. Yet O- ye bleffed Saints and Angels (if ye can behold fuch Worfhippers as thefe men) fee with what wicked Plots and bloody hands they offer Incenfe : Can ye poffibly accept their Prayers. No, none can ac- cept them but their own *Martyrs*. But all Worfhip (how innocent foever) is rejected in Heaven, where the God of it alone is not fought to : therefore the right ask- ing of *Life* is from him, who can onely give *Grace*, and lift us up to his own *Glory*.

III. The third and laft way we are to confider him is, As a *Worker*, *in that he has made the Doctrine of Eternal Life effectual to Salvation.*

For this *Word* (He has commiſ-ſion'd us to preach) is the great Inſtrument of the New-birth : It is a means to beget in us a *true Faith* , and being once ſtedfaſtly embraced , it gives us the firſt-fruits of Eternal Life , till we are fully inveſted in the Inheritance. What was heretofore the vertue of his *Word* at the creation of all things, when he ſpoke out a World, and call'd it forth into an actual Being, the ſame is the vertue of his written Word , whereby he calls Us to an Eternal one. For the *All-quickning Spirit* is mixt with it ; whence it becoms fruitfully ſtrong and mighty to ſave thoſe that hear. What Rock is there ſo hard, or Ground ſo barren,that can reſiſt the influence of its power ? How does it cut through a *heart of ſtone* , and

cultivate the *Defart* of *wild pafsions*!
How does it mould and fafhion us
to become a people acceptable to
the Lord! If natural inclination
or carnal intereft fhould ftand up
to oppofe it, thefe are but like
Muddy Fortreffes that are quickly
batter'd and diffolv'd ; and a new
frame is fet up in the foul, that is
pure and heavenly ; which expref-
fes the Agent in the *Divinity* of his
work, and fhows the beauty of
thofe *Promifes* he applies, in fuch
motions that bend wholly towards
them. This Spirit of old (which
worked by the Word) drew multitudes of men to Chriftianity,
beating down in them the ftrong
holds of fin and Satan, fanctifying
their natures, and fo giving them
a new relifh of things ; raifing
their love to a Chrift crucified,
and their defires after a diftant reward ; whence they would not fo
much

much as receive *their good things
here*, in hopes of a *richer treafure
hereafter*. Truly even the Word it
felf did much perfwade : but the
Spirit came in with a *Demonftration*;
whereby they gave up their private interefts, furrendred their
darling lufts, and cafting out every
thing that refifted, yielded themfelves abfolutely to his conduct.

Thefe things confidered, who
can deny the *fulnefs* of his *Miniftry*,
that fees Heaven and Hell in their
diftinct lights fet before him, which
heretofore were either *quencht* by
Fables, or under *Shadows conceal'd?*
Who can deny the *right* of his *Purchafe*, that beholds the merit of
his Sufferings, for which his Humane nature was lifted up, and ve-
fted in full power to fit on the
Throne and pronounce *life* to his
followers ? As little can we deny
the Third way, namely the *Effi-*
cacy

cacy of his *Doctrine* to lead us thither, if we either reflect upon it as the Power of God, or the natural tendency of it to work in us a spirit of Holinefs, and fo fit us for Glory. Thefe things *St. Peter* had refpect to when he fo emphatically tells his Mafter, *Thou haft the words of eternal life.*

This-Phrafe (*Eternal Life*) is a fhort defcription of the good mans future eftate; nor is it otherwife ever mentioned in Scripture than as fignifying the Saints Portion: fo that for Chrift to have *words* of that kind, is to have in ftore for him a double Blefling: For when He fpeaks *life*, he puts him into *poffeßion* of an *Inheritance*; when he fpeaks an *Eternal Life*, he gives him a *fecurity* of *enjoying* : whence he mercifully joyns them in his Sentence of blifs, as they are necefarily joyn'd in the notion.

I

I shall not trouble my Reader with a farther Comment, nor run into a controversie whether there be indeed such an estate that we from Scripture are assur'd Christ speaks of, it being no way pertinent to this Text I discuss, nor I presume to him that peruses it; of whom I ought to suppose that Principles are believed, which neither imply in them a contradiction for *Reason* to cavil at, nor hazard for *Wisdom* to fear.

It remains I should show the force of the Argument why we should stick close to our Lord and Master from *St. Peters* supposition that the Doctrine of *Eternal Life* proceeds from him.

It were much to be wish'd that the rules he lays down for our Course upon earth might bind followers to him without such a proposal as that is; since they yield

us

us a prefent pay in *Honour, Eafe,*
and *Pleafure,* that do certainly wait
upon vertuous actions: But if Flefh
be fo ftrong as to reject thofe motives by reafon of the narrownefs
of their limits, how can we exclude an *Eternity* of all thefe, where
it adds another Good, *fafety* to
perfect them? Behold! there is in
that ftate of Eternal Life a compleat anfwer to thofe two Paf-
fions that govern us here, and
make our life a torment to us except they be fatisfied.   For

  1. The Gift is fo vaft that it
fwallows up Hope.

  2. So durable that it removes
Fear.

  Now in all *Hope* there is want,
and *defire* is nothing elfe but a *cra-*
ving emptinefs in the *Soul.* That
hungry Gueft is often call'd to an
Epicures Feaft, and as often fpoils it,
turning his *Plenty* into *Penance* fince

                                        it

it cannot fill. The like vanity of Imperfection cleaves to other worldly enjoyments, becaufe the eye of our mind (being too big for them) has an unquiet Appetite of looking farther. But it is impoffi-ble there fhould be any place for that reftlefs Paffion where an *In-finite Good* is injoyed: For this is an Object which tranfcends even our thoughts, furpaffes our fancies that our defires are founded on, and fo delightfully keeps us within its *Circle* : All that we can imagine is there prefent, and therefore all we can *hope for* has in that prefence an *end.* Hence we come fettled to thofe Joys, and bring a fpirit full and entire to feed on them : fo that there is no colour for a depar-ture to a leffer Good, that leaves us ftill diffatisfied in our fruition. Such are all Temporal Objects we purfue: they naturally tempt us to

fall

fall off from that chafe, becaufe
they do not anfwer our expectation, I mean while another is in
our view, that (being eternal)
commands our defires, fulfils our
hopes, and cures the defect of both
with the fatisfying widenefs of its
compafs.

Next for *Fear* : this infeparably
attends us in life; and argues not
onely *want and emptinefs*, but the
mifery and pain of it.　*Hope* may af-
flict us for the abfence of a Good,
but then it fome way chears us
for the likelihood of attaining it;
but *Fear* is a paffion that eats into
our delights, and devours all our
Contentments. Neither can we
poffibly be freed from it, while
we reflect upon thofe changes
which the *Stage* of this World ex-
pofes us to; States and Kingdoms
being fhifted there like *Scenes*, and
almoft with the fame *quicknefs*.

I.　　　　　But

But the Doctrine of *Eternal Life* (Chrift promifes) is a Soveraign remedy againft all trouble ; for it fhows us a *fixt point*, an *unchangeable inftant* ; nor can we be afraid with that contemplation, no more than we are with the profpect of Shores and Havens, that receive us fafe from a Storm. How is the foul quieted to think that thofe evils it fuffers are pafling away, and a fettled reft is prepared! With what peace does it apprehend a moments danger when a perfect Liberty is the recompence! This and much more does a *bleft Eternity* import, and through that encouragement is a Chriftian arm'd to encounter any affliction.

And fo we read what a ftoutnefs of fpirit was rais'd in the Primitive Profeffors, that preach'd up Chriftianity and ventur'd all upon it. A bare Faith did not carry them

to

to that act, but a Faith that was grounded upon the Heavenliness of the *Doctrine*, Courage of *Martyrs*, and Power of *Miracles*; strong Promises that will infer as strong Conclusions, except wee'l say Heaven and Earth were combin'd together in a plot to abuse, and the abuse too must be this, *viz.* a *cheating* of an *Idolatrous world* into *good living*. Let the Scoffer count it madnels to quit *Sense* for a Good that is yet hid from him; I could tell him that even a *Present Good* is *invisible*; for we want time to discern it for its *shortness*, we want a Substance to be discern'd for its *emptiness*; whereas an *eternal* one is *invisible* for its *transcendent fulness*. Thither does right Reason drive us, and a true principle of Self-love, it being our interest to seek a Treasure that will not fail us.

But should we take the opposite state to This Life, namely *E-ternal Death* which is the Curse he threatens to those that deny him) here we are ty'd to our Masters service by a sure chain, which the dread of Omnipotence puts on. Earthly Powers can awe their Subjects, and justly too, with what they are able outwardly to inflict; yet Death (being the utmost stroke of that Justice) seems indeed but a retreat from it. But the *Grave* (how free and quiet soever it be) is no Sanctuary to keep us from Gods hand : It dissolves our *Bodies*, but not his *Government*; who watches every particle of our dust, and locks it up safe for an after-summons; but the Soul He makes ~~the~~ the immediate subject of his Tribunal. Therefore the highest homage may be well demanded of us, upon whom the highest Soveraignty is shown.

I

I confeſs none come up from the dead to tell us this news : no, they cannot ; for the Judges Sentence binds them to their ſeats, where their great part is ſuffering ; and if they could , 'tis uſeleſs , no ways tending to ſettle our Faith, but rather confirming our ſuſpicion that in Satans Errand ſome *Ghoſt* may be employed. If *Scripture* (which *St. Peter* calls a *light that ſhineth in a dark place*) be with all its evidence of Divine Witneſſes diſown'd, how can we believe a teſtimony from the *Damn'd*, that would be ſure to bring with them all their *night to deceive* ? This then can be no objection. The true one is form'd by our own corrupt hearts ; and we are apt to queſtion the Evilday , becauſe we would not be checkt nor controll'd in our ſinning. In the mean time we baffle that deſign by ſtarting ſuch a

I 3 doubt ;

doubt; which unfettling the foul in its pleafures, does thereby hinder it from enjoying them. ↓ We labour to be *Scepticks* that we may offend, and after we are fo, we find our felves pain'd with that Uncertainty. Oh let us be wife for our latter end, and choofe to ferve our God by a true Faith, fince our endeavouring to fhake it does but wake Confcience to torture us.

Hitherto I have handled the *Argument St. Peter* lays down for following his *Lord*, and by the way toucht upon the Sinners *Judgment* : I have fhown the *noblenefs* of *Faith*, the *authority* of *Truth*, and the *excellent manner* of revealing it by Chrift above all thofe difcoveries that were made : The natural refult from all is this, that we would ferioufly inquire whether we can better our life under another fervice, and if that be not poffible, then

then immediately lift our felves his Difciples in all the watchful-nefs of Devotion.

As to the matter of *Inquiry*, it becomes us as men not to take any Mafter upon truft, or the cuftome of others : Credulity is proper to Children that are weak and want finews; but the ftrength of Wif-dom confifts in this, *to prove all things*, and not be eafily govern'd in our actings. Yet this childifh weaknefs are moft men fubject to in their main end, when they re-linquifh their own Faculties that would lead them to Chriftianity ; and fuffer themfelves to be led by a Cuftomary Dilcipline that de-ftroys it. What that teaching is, and how far it extends , every one knows : The mind is not taught here , but the *brutifh part* and fome *tranfient reward* pro-pounded to encourag it : Tran-

fient

sient I call it with respect to those two *Masters* that rule over us, *Flesh* and the *World*, which pretend to nothing higher in their offers of Good; for all the colour they have to invite us is only the gratifying of our senses for a few moments; onely *Satan* makes bold to counterfeit our Lord, and wears his shape in a *full promise*, that so his hook may the better faften and catch our appetite when he tempts us.   He has therefore in readiness for his followers *words of Eternal Life* (as he had for *Eve*) but those very words prove fatal; for with the same breath he kills the Sholar that hears him. What other effect can be look'd for from a *Serpent condemn'd*? who delights in the spreading of his plague, and knows no other liberty from torment, than that pleasure he takes in enlarging his *Hell*.   To this end he

con-

continues down the poyſon of that Doctrine (*Eat and live, ſin and be happy*) in the mouths of his *Falſe-Prophets;* who are very buſie to re-concile Faith with an Evil Conſcience , and would fain compound up a *Religion of Fleſh;* which are arts indeed to draw many after them in regard they *bribe* their Senſuality : But let us ſee the iſſue of all this, and what fruit there is in obeying ſuch Doctrines, when the Good (there promiſed) is *blown a-way* with our *breath,* and inſtead of light we find darkneſs.

On the contrary under Chriſts rule we have an *Eternal Life* ten-dred to us in all certainty ; and the condition He requires of us is an excellent part of that *Life,* ſince it gives us a proper *Eye* to enjoy it : The condition I mean is Purity of Heart, a Grace that doubly profits the Soul, firſt in *refining* our natures, next

next in *ſrengthening* us to *ſee* Glory.
Who would not endeavour to be
thus qualified for Heaven? Can
any corruption move us to forfeit
Security? and can there be greater
ſecurity than the Good here promiſed? Mans *Knowledge* you will
grant is much *exalted* in *foreſeeing*
future things, but his *Reaſon* is
more *advanc'd* in *purſuing* them.
And whither would we go from
our Lord? Other Offerers of happineſs do betray us; He onely can
ſave. To him Nature has ſubje-
cted us as being made; Gratitude
as being redeem'd; Intereſt as ex-
pecting a reward : ſo that to deny him our hearts is to joyn Sacrilege and folly together, when
we rob God and impoveriſh our
ſelves.

We are all covetous of *Life,* and
of Life too in its beſt eſtate. For
though ſin has corrupted mens
choice

choice of the *way*, yet it has not blafted their defires of the end. But our Lord has farther provided thofe defires fhould not be fruftra- ted, if we follow his rule, and ftrictly adhere to his Commands in *mortifying* our *affections and lufts*, and as it were *fpiritnallizing* the *whole man* to be thereby fitted for his Kingdom. It is from us he expects this work fhould be performed, and not from *age*: Age may indeed prove the *mortifier* of a *Luft*, but withall it *kills* the *fervice*. Little is the glory of overcoming the *Temp- ter* when he does not affault us ; but to break flefhly motions in all their ftrength this is a true Con- queft. Neither fhould it be thought ftrange for any Difciple to deny thus *felf* in Chriftianity ; for *Hea- ven* being the object of that work will eafily deftroy the Miracle of doing it. How can any of us con- template

template the happiness above, and yet not be willing to forſake his proper ſins, ſins (how colour'd ſoever) yet in the midſt of their *Varniſh* deform'd ! Where is true beauty but that of *Life*, which only in the *Counterfeit* we admire ? where is true wealth but that of *Immortality*, which only in the *Glitter* we eſteem ! ſince then ſuch a fair and ſubſtantial Treaſure is there offer'd us, we ought like wiſe-men to determine our choice ; and forſaking the vanities of other objects, become fixt and ſettled in our endeavours, that we may obtain and compaſs that Good which yields ſo bright, ſo weighty, ſo glorious a recompence to the Purſuer.

The

The Fourth Difcourfe.

Rom. 8. 34.

Who is he that condemneth? It is Chrift that died, yea rather that is rifen again.

THe *Juftification* of a Sinner, and the way God has pre-fcribed to fave men by, is fo miftaken in the world, that no Point has begot more difputes, nor is there any Theme wherein Scripture has more fuffer'd. Yet this *quarrel* amongft men cannot be charg'd upon any want of evidence in this particular; but either an *humour of pride* to contradict, or the *intereft of a Party* to purfue, or the *prejudice of Opinion* to defend, have been

been the main caufe of that contention. Would we come with a
fincere mind to the reading of the
Word, efpecially the Writings of
this *Apoftle*, we fhould find the
difficulty of that *Truth* clear'd, and
the glorious effects of *Chrifts Me-
diatorfhip* laid open, upon which
our *Juftifying* does depend.

Now for the better handling
this Text (which I have here chofen to difcufs) I fhall a little explain the verfe before it, by reafon
of their neceffary connexion together. In which verfe we may obferve

1. The Triumphant Challenge
he makes, fummoning any Adverfary to appear in *Court* τίς ἐγκαλέσει
Who will charge or accufe ?

2. The Ground of his confidence how little that *Accufation*
would avail, becaufe of the mercy of the Judge that *acquits* the
offen-

offendor.--- *It is God that justifies.*

3. The limitation of the *Charge* in respect of the party against whom it is drawn, and the limitation of the act of *Justifying Grace* in respect of the party to whom it belongs----*Who will lay any thing to the charge of Gods elect?* It *is God that justifies,* that is those *Elect* : where by Gods *Elect* he means the same that are spoken of in the first verse of the Chapter, namely such as *are in Christ Jesus, that walk not after the Flesh, but after the Spirit* : that is, who perform all the conditions required in the *New Covenant* : For these alone are the chosen of God, whom He has decreed to reward with Eternal Life.

But because the grace of *Justification* does necessarily suppose a work of *Satisfaction* (since the goodness of God could have no place for *justifying* a sinner, were not the way

way firſt made by *attoning* his *Ju-*
ſtice) he therefore proceeds in my
Text to clear that point, and ſhow
whence *Pardoning Mercy* ſprings,
namely from Chriſts undertaking
our Cauſe, and reconciling us to his
Father by the vertue of his Media=
torſhip. He indeed is the *Stone* upon
which all our ſalvation is built, ſo
that without him there neither is
nor can be given either Pardon of
ſin here, or Glory hereafter. Hence
the *Apoſtle* with regard to his *ſatis-*
faction does further urge, and more
ſtrongly confirm what he laid
down in the former verſe, *Who is he*
that condemneth? it is Chriſt that died,
yea rather that is riſen again.

The words contain in them a
True Believers *full diſcharge* ; and
the *Reaſon* or Ground of it. The
fulneſs of the diſcharge is held
forth in that Queſtion, *Who is he*
that condemneth? The reaſon of it

is

Acts 4. 11,
12.

is expreſt in that double work of our Redeemer, but one of them more dignified than the other. *It is Chriſt that died ; yea, rather is riſen again.*

The ſenſe of the whole may be reſolv'd into theſe Three Propoſitions.

1. That there is a Proper and Peculiar Vertue to be aſcribed to Chriſts *Death* in the act of redeeming us.

2. That there are Proper and Peculiar Advantages in Chriſts *Ri-ſing* above that Death.

3. That Chriſts *Death* in particular, but more eminently his *Ri-ſing*, has procur'd the Saints freedom from Condemnation.

I. *That there is a Proper and Peculiar Vertue to be aſcribed to Chriſts Death in the act of Redeeming us.*

In the handling of it I ſhall premiſe ſome Truths.

K   *Firſt,*

First, I take for granted what Scripture so clearly reveals, that the breach of a *Positive Law* (which was given to *Adam* in *Paradise*) did not onely involve him but his Posterity too in the Curse there threatned; so that the propagation of *Mankind* from him was but the propagation of *persons condemn'd*; all of us being lyable thereby to *Death Temporal and Eternal.*

Secondly, though God considered in his *Absolute Power* could *forgive* Man the sin he had committed, yet considered in the *Decree* he had made of punishing his Sin, and as a *Governour* bound to maintain it, so he was *hindred* from the exercise of that power.

Thirdly, No creature could possibly reverse that *Decree*, nor expiate the violation of this *Governours Authority*, for want of a Satisfaction which He demanded. For

where

where was the Creature that could give it ? *Angels* withdraw from the *brightnefs* of Gods *Glory*, how then would they flee from the *Fire* of his *wrath* ! *Man* cannot bear the punifhment due to one of his *own* , how then would he fuftain the *fins* of a *World* ! Had either of them been deputed to this Task, they had funk under it, poor Mankind had been loft, and God ftill unreconcil'd : For to the work of Satisfying him *Srength* as well as *Innocence* is required ; but the Creature at beft is too *weak* to *intercede* ; the *price* of its fuffering too *mean*, the merit of which cannot extend to another; and fo Divine Juftice inftead of accepting would quite *devour* the *Sacrifice*.

Therefore it was neceffary to our recovery one fhould undertake for us, that could anfwer the rigour of the *Decree* by his *Sufferings*,

K 2   and

and fupply the defects both of Men and Angels by the *Innocence* and *Worth* of a Sacrifice; *Innocence* to *prepare,* and *Worth* to *crown* the *Oblation.*

Now that Chrift was thus qualified to appear in our ftead, may be eafily evinc'd , if we will but confider either the purity of his *Humane nature*, which was *without ſpot* , or the *Majeſty of his Perſon,* who is *God bleſſed for ever.* The firft of thefe would ferve to make his *Offering holy*; the latter would give it *infinite value*; by both which he was fitted to pay our debt, and bear all the wrath of his Father due to our fins.

And that He actually did what He was fo qualified to perform , we have the like evidence from Scripture. The whole Oeconomy of the *Jews* , and the ftrain of the *Goſpel* confirms it. The Sacrifices of

1 Pet. 1. 19.
Rom. 9. 5.

of the Old Law were Types and *dark Images* of this Great one that was *once* to be offered for the fins of the people : The Gofpel-phrafe points altogether to this Truth ; and therefore when it fpeaks of Chrift, it calls him λύ7ρον a *price of ranfome*, nay ἀν7ίλυ7ρον, that is a price by way of *exchange*, in *fupplying our place* : again we are faid to be *ju-ftified by his Blood, reconciled through his Death*, and to have *redemption* by his *Sufferings* : all which expreffi-ons fignifie the *proper effeЄt of his Death* was the *remiſſion of our fins.* This He himfelf teftifies, how that his *Blood was ſhed for the remiſſion of fins* ; whence we may take comfort in his Death, and rejoyce in the vertue of his Attonement, where-by our *pardon* is obtain'd.

Mat. 20. 28.

1 Tim. 2. 6.

Matt. 26. 28.

Should we now with the *Soci-nian* make plain words that exprefs all this, to be meer *Metaphors* and

K 3   *Figures,*

Figures, we may as well joyn with the old *Hereticks* (the *Valentinians*) that made a *Figure* of his *Living*, *Dying* and *Rising*; in that they denied the reality of his *Flesh*: nor can their Opinion be more contrary to the Faith than this: For as to hold He was but the *Image* of a *Man* deſtroys a *Chriſt*, ſo to hold He was but the *Image* of a *Prieſt* deſtroys a *Saviour*. Thus to wreſt the Scripture is to wreſt it to our deſtruction : for what follows upon it ? If he be not in a true ſenſe *offer'd* for us, we are ſtill in our ſins, the Curſe of the Law yet abides, and his Death becomes altogether unprofitable, when it brings us deliverance but in *ſhadow*. I might add how his ſuffering upon any other account than in our *ſtead* to redeem us, has nothing of juſtice in it, and therefore cannot demonſtrate the juſtice of another;

other ; whereas *his Blood and the* Rom.3.25.
declaring of Gods righteoufnefs are
joyned together : but if He who
was all innocence in himfelf, did
not bear our guilt when He fuffer'd, the Death He underwent
(being properly a punifhment becaufe *fins wages*) would be fo far
from declaring Gods righteoufnefs,
that it could onely manifeft the
Tyranny of the Inflicter.

Yet thefe kind of men are the
great pretenders to *Reafon*, who
reject the Doctrine of *Satisfaction*;
but cannot maintain what they de-
liver without laying their ground-
work in *impiety*; which is to affert
He was no *God* that fuffer'd; where
how grofly they renounce their
reafon will appear in this, that
denying him to be God, they deny themfelves to be True Worfhippers, and proclaim to the
world their *Idolatry* in *adoring Man*.

K 4 But

But their abfurdity farther appears, when denying the Meritorioufnefs of his *Satisfaction* , they can yet make his Sufferings to be meritorious of *Divine Power*; as if there were any proportion betwixt meer humane actions and fo high a reward. Now what Merit is this that could raife him to be the *Head of Angels*, and Governour of all created Beings ; nay to be adored and worfhipped *equally* with the *Father*; which *Honours* the collected fervices of the whole Creation cannot reach to ? May not the Heathens fcoff at their Idolatry, who pretending to Chriftianity, fet up a *made God* to pray to ; and expect Salvation from One who is *exalted* for the vertue of his fufferings in maintaining his *Religion* , as *they confecrated* theirs for the Gallantry of publick actions ? Behold ! this is onely to refine,

fine, but not to change the nature of Gentilism : as likewise it utterly overthrows the *Mystery of Godliness*, and destroys the *Greatness of Divine Love*; which consisted chiefly in abasing the *Deity* for Mans sake, whereas this makes it ridiculous and dishonourable in thus exalting the *Humanity*.

But I leave them to their Judg above, and their Books to Judges below : I shall now onely briefly inquire into Two things for the better opening this Point, and so proceed to my Second Observable.

1. How Chrifts Death is the Cause of the remission of our fins.

2. From what Time we should date the Benefit of that remission, as it is made ours.

1. *How Chrifts Death is the Cause,* &c.---- I answer thus; God the Father was mov'd for that *price* his

Son

Son layd down (which was his precious Blood) to free us from that punishment we deserved in our own persons; and to enter in= to a New Covenant with us; offering us *Pardon of sin and Eternal Life* upon new easie terms of *faith and sincere obedience* : whereas before rigorous Justice bore the sway, and shut us all up under a a sentence of condemnation without hope of mercy. Therefore He is called the *Mediator of a better Co= venant ;* and whereas in the old League we were used as *Gibeonites* and made *slaves,* in this New one (procured by Christ) we are treated as a *free People,* and made capable of the Privileges of his Kingdome. This He ratified in his own *Blood* ; whence his Blood is called the *Blood of the New Testament ,* wherein all his promises of Grace are confirm'd, and the *Legal Curse* done away. See

See here the Love of a *Saviour*, that would thus die to reftore us; buy our peace at the price of himfelf, and bring us terms of falvation fo dearly purchafed, which before we could not hope for. This fhows the wretchednefs of our ftate, and the need we ftòod in of fuch an *Expiation*, when He who could *create* us at firft with the *eafe* of a *word*, is not allowed to create us anew but with the *pain* of *fuffering*. The Crofs upon which He did this work, is a fad fpectacle to *Senfe*, but a glad object of *Faith* : the one prefents him *naked* in our *Flefh*, but the other *covered* with our *Sins*; the one fhows him in his *Blood*, but the other in our *Guilt*, the burden of which He carried up thither, encountred his Fathers wrath, and at the very point of death proclaimed his Victory, *It is finifhed*; which is

all

all one with this, The *Attonement is wrought*, becaufe the *Victim* is flain.

2. *From what time we ſhould date the Benefit of that Remiſſion, when it is made ours?* I anſwer not immediately from his Satisfaction, but from the time of our *rightly believing* in him. *We are juſtified by his Blood* in one ſenſe, and *we are juſtified by faith in his Blood* in another : His bloody Death procur'd for us the *Pardon*, which is nothing elſe but putting us into *capacity* of being *pardoned;* but *True Faith applies* the Pardon to the Soul, whereby we *actually enjoy it.* How Faith here will be underſtood, may be found out by comparing two places of Scripture, namely *Acts* 10. 43. with *Acts* 3. 19. In the one it is ſaid, *Whoſoever believeth in him ſhall receive remiſſion of ſins :* in the other, *Repent and be converted, that your ſins may be blotted out :* ſo that True

Faith

Faith is the Principle of a new life, the beginning of *Sanctification*; when the Heart is resign'd up to God, and with sincere resolutions turns to him. No Faith can *justifie* us but as Faith that thus worketh: for as God will take no unsanctified person to his Glory, so neither will He seal to him in that condition *pardon of sin* here, which is the earnest of that Glory.

Trust not then to his *Wounds* if thou bearest not the *marks* of them in thy *Soul*; rely not on his Death, if sin in thee be not crucified. They were Reprobate Jews that turn'd his Passion into a *Sight*, and came off not wounded; but true Christians are *pierced* with *beholding* him, and find it operative upon their lives. Should we be *justified* without doing any thing on our part, obedience to Gods Commands would rather be a *Gift* than a *Debt*;

a *Debt*; whereas the Gospel en-
joyns it us as *necessary* to please
Him; let us then so come to his
Grave, as not idly to *bury* our
selves there; for we are but *dead
men* in doing so; neither will our
Master be found, since the Angel
can tell us, *He is not there but is risen;*
whence we ought not to rest in
that place, but go forth to *seek* him.
All the vertue that is in the *Sepulcher* comes out to those that *rise* and
resemble him who is risen, *That
like as he was raised from the dead by
the glory of the Father, so they likewise
might walk in newness of life.* Thus
much for the First Observable.

 I proceed to handle the Second
Proposition.

 II. *That there are proper and peculiar Advantages in Christs rising a-
bove that death---- yea rather is risen
again.*

 All the time Christ slept in the
Grave

Grave was a time of gloominefs and thick darknefs : but here God fpeaks as he did in the old Creation, *Let there be light* : His *rifing* bring us *day* and the joyes of it ; wherein *Death* has loft all its *fpoyls*, and *Life* his *victory* ; *Sin* has fpent all its *force*, and *Mercy triumphs* ; the *Synagogue* it felf *ends*, and our *Church* begins. A Day very pleafant in the fpeculation ! but may no doubt come in, that it is artificially fram'd and devifed by Chriftians? Truly doubts cannot be hindred, where corruption and infidelity fo much reigns ; but the reafon of our doubting is taken away by the clear *evidence* that is given us of his *Refurrection.*

If you ask *what that is,* behold ! it is grounded upon *Prophets* that *fortell* ; *Eye-witneffes* that *confirm*, and *God* himfelf *attefting* the truth of both by the power of his *Spirit* that

that worked in the Preachers, to make this Point undeniable. To the *Prophets* St. *Peter* appeals for convincing the *Jews*; and St. *Paul* makes it a ftanding proof, how He *rofe again according to the Scriptures.* *Eye-witneſſes* are produc'd to convince the *Gentiles,* not onely a few Women and Apoftles whom he had chofen, but *Five hundred Bre-thren at once* : and thofe He ap= pear'd to were not fo much confi-derable for their number as for their *nicety* in believing; men that had fcruples of *fenfe* which kept them from being *deceived,* as well as fcruples of *concience,* which kept them from *deceiving* others. The firft of thefe is manifeft from hence, That they would not thoroughly believe *He was rifen* (though they faw him) till they were convinc'd by the very *touch* : the latter is cleer from that *Doctrine* they em= braced,

Acts 2.

1 Cor. 15. 4.

braced, which forbad the *leaft fin*; and how can we imagine they durft propagate a *Cheat* under all difcouragements, when they knew they not onely ran the hazard of lofing their Lives (as they did by profeffing him) but their Hopes too of a better life (the onely *An= chor* of their Profeffion) from which a *Lye* would certainly exclude them. Add to this the *Spirit* they received, the Wonders they wrought, and the *Succefs* they had in their *Miniftry*, when their Doctrine fpread through the world from poor naked beginnings meer= ly by the force of this *Article*, it fhows the Body of their Mafter was not ftoln away (as the Keep= ers *abfurdly* reported) but that God himfelf was *rifen* to defend them. Thefe things well confi= der'd (if they amount not to *De-*

L   *mon-*

monſtration) yet afford ſo *rational a proof*, as will engage our aſſent to the Truth, and convince us of folly in denying it.

Now the Advantages of Chriſts *Riſing* above *his Death* have a double aſpect; for they either relate to Chriſt or to Us.

Firſt to Chriſt, and ſo the Dignity of his Reſurrection is ſeen in, theſe Particulars.

1. It juſtiſied the *Innocence* of his *Humanity*.

When Chriſt was laid hold of, and carried away to be condemn'd by the *Jews*, then his very *Cauſe* ſeem'd to be given up : It was counted criminal with them that He would ſubmit to an *Arreſt*, and a ſufficient evidence to make him a Malefactor, that He did ſo tamely yield to the *Trial*. But when He endured the *Sentence* to be

be pronounced, went patiently to
his *Crofs*, and fuffer'd his Body to
be faftned with the *nails*, as if He
had the *guilt* of a *Slave* with the
punifhment , here was the *Hour* to
overcome Truth, and the *Power of
darknefs* to cover him , who is *the
light of the world.*

But his *Rifing from death* removed that *Eclipfe*, cleard that *Inno-
tence*, by the *diftinction* it made of
his *Fate*, when the Vilenefs of his
Execution gave Authority to the
Charge. This caufed fuch bold-
nefs in *Peter* to plead for his Mafter, and return the fault upon his
Perfecutors (which He was fo
guilty of himfelf) *Ye have denyed* Acts 3. 14.
the holy one and the juft ; and he proceeds farther to aggravate their
Crime, and maintain the righteoufnefs of his Caufe by that convincing Argument *of Gods raifing* Verf. 15.
him

him from the dead. Now it is easie for any one to conclude, that had our Lord been an Impostor, or an evil doer, he could not rise; such kind of men would surely rot in the Grave, and know no other Resurrection than that of the last Day to a worse Judgment; because for God to *punish* them with *Death here,* and allow them presently to *rise,* that so they might confirm their own followers in those Errors they taught, and those Evils they practised; here a work of *Divinity* would be employed to destroy the true worship of it, which is a flat contradiction to his Goodness. Christ therefore by his *rising* had a Testimony from Heaven of his uprightness, and the *Evidence seal'd by Omnipoteoce* it self, That He was the True Prophet which came into the world.   2. It

2. It declared the Divinity of his Power; *For He raised up him-self.* Now to *raise the Dead* is beyond the ſtrength of a *Finite Agent*; and to *reſtore* things as well as *create* them does equally require an *Almighty hand*; both which works not being to be found in *Nature,* the *Heathens* (thence taking their meaſures) judg'd them *Impoſſible* to be done : which is an *unreaſon-able* limiting of the *God* of *Nature,* when Men will not conſider what *reſerves* of *Power* He ought to have that is the Fountain of all the acti-ons of his Creatures.

That Chriſt would thus raiſe up himſelf, He in his life-time foretold, and He particularly ap-peals to the Divinity of that act (He would one day ſhow) as a ſign of his Authority to purge that *Temple* which they profan'd. And 2 Joh. 19.

L 3   the

the Apostle *S.Paul* expresly tells us
Rom. 1.4. how *by his resurrection from the dead
He was declared to be the Son of God
with power*; that is with power He
had in *himself* to *give life*, not with
power his Father alone put forth
in quickning him; for then his
Rising would be common to him
with others. But did not the Miracles He wrought (when living)
declare him likewise to be the
Son of God? Not so convincingly
as this : for the Wonders He then
did, meer men (such were the
Prophets) had the Priviledg of doing before him; but none except
the *Son of God* could thus *rise*;
much less did his *dying* reveal him
in that Majesty, which could only declare him to be the *Son of
Man* with *weakness.* For what
more argues it then to *dye?* what
greater scandal of that weakness
than

than to die on the *Crofs* ? wherein
the *Godhead* ftooped to the loweft
infirmities of Flefh, and the worft
malice of his Perfecutors. Then
his Enemies could grow bold, and
fcoffingly demand fome proof of
his Power, and the contemptible-
nefs of that ftate He was in (which
hid all his Greatnefs) made them
ask fuch a fign of it as that was of
faving himfelf; which, if granted,
had kept the world from being
fayed.

But his *Rifing from death* had all
marks of glory in it ; the *breaking
up* of the *Sepulcher* , the *Miniftry of
Angels* , the *fhaking of Earth* , and
the trembling of Keepers ; which were
but feveral wayes of *Homage* due
to the *Power* of his *Refurreftion.*
Here He difcovered himfelf to be
truly God, and confirm'd the Faith
of his Difciples with the Reafon
L 4 they

they had to worſhip him :

3. It inveſted him in his Rights, and put him into actual poſſeſſion of his Kingdom.

This was the *Covenant* betwixt Him and his Father, that He ſhould firſt make Attonment for ſin by his Death, and receive afterwards the reward of that work in *Dominion.* Hence we read how Phil. 2.9. *for becoming obedient to Death, even the Death of the Croſs; He was therefore highly exalted ; for drinking of* Pſa.110.7. *the brook of the way he ſhould therefore lift up his head.* King He was indeed from his very birth, but He receiv'd not then *the oyl of gladneſs above his fellows :* the Honour of his Anointing was as imperfect as the Form He aſſum'd, which was the Form of a Servant, where He was put under ſubjection to the Law and the Curſe, but after

He

He *rofe* ἐτελειώθη, He was *made per-feƈ*, that is, *aƈtually crown'd.* This is that παλιγγενεσία, the *Regeneration* or New *ƒtate* mention'd, namely the Kingdom of the Meſſiah, which takes its date from the time of his *Reſurreƈtion;* for then He ſhowed his Conqueſt of the chief Rebel *Satan,* by overturning the *Foundation* of his Empire, which was laid in the *Grave;* ſo that whereas all other Princes Glory ends in. that place, this Princes *Triumph* there began; then He commiſſioned his Diſciples to Preach every where and Baptize, to gather him a *Church* made up of Jews and Gentiles, where He would alwayes rule and preſide, when as before they continued Members of the *Synagogue.* And his Authority to do this He grounds upon that *Univerſal power that was given him both*

Matt. 19. 28.

Mat. 28.

in

in Heaven and in Earth, whereto He had *right* in his Flefh as the *Heir*, but the *exercife* of it as a *Poffeffor* was fufpended till his rifing.

Should we compare his condition under death with this his condition after it, we fhall find a vaft difference; for at his death He was fo far from having the Enfigns of Soveraignty, that He bore onely the looks and wore the chains of a Captive : The great mark of his Kingfhip appear'd in the *Title* of his *Charge, King of the Jews*; which being fet over his head, and He crucified under it, it fhowed He was the object more of mens Mockery than Fear. But when He *rofe*, He put on Greatnefs, took the *Scepter* in his *hand*, and made his *way* as a *Prince* by *victory*. Here He manifefted the Vertue of his *Kingly Office*, and con-

convinc'd the World of his right to command, and what obedience is due to his Laws.

Hitherto I have insisted upon the *Dignity* of the *Resurrection* as it relates to *Christ*, I shall next consider the Advantages of it as it relates to us--- *Yea rather is risen again.* And they are these:

1. It manifested a full discharge of our *Debt*, and Gods ready accepting of that price which was paid.

When a *Surety* that undertakes anothers Debt is cast into *prison* by the *Creditor*, if he comes out of it, it argues the *Creditor* is fully satisfied : so Christs coming out of the *Grave* (whether He was delivered by the Judg for our offences) declares the obligation is taken off, and no more left for Him to suffer. To this purpose the Apostle

speaks

Rom.4.25. speaks, *That He rose again for our Justification,* or in other terms, to give us *assurance* by the *Satisfaction* of his *Death* that our *Acquittance* is obtain'd. The work of Redemption was perform'd in the *dark* when *He dyed*; all the time He was held in the Grave, we could have no sense of a deliverance; but when He who was *slain* for a *Sin-offering,* presented himself afterwards *alive* before the Lord, this brought us *light* to behold the *Perfection* of that Attonement.

Look then on his *Death* as the cause of thy *freedom*, but on his *Rising* as the ground of thy *comfort* : in the one He was the *Priest* to *offer,* in the other the *Messenger* to *assure* us ; a preceding requisite to give us the joy of a Saviour, and compleat our notion of his performance, when we should see

his

his love in the *strength* of it, find
out the *Price* He laid down for us
by *Death* in the *Power* of that Evidence He gave us by *Life.* The
Scape-goat under the Law was but
a poor *uncomfortable Type*, that had
all the iniquities, sins, and tranfgreffions of Israel put upon his
head, and was after this sent a-
way into the Wilderness, whence
he never return'd : but Chrift
that bore the sins of the World,
and entred the *Wilderness* not in-
habited (*the Grave*) came out
thence to bring us the news of his
Expiation, and so made us certain
of the benefit. It was not enough
with him to work our Redemption, except we were further enlightned to know it : Thus He
doubled the mercy of that act,
when we whofe ftate He recover'd by dying, had our *Fears*
too

too *heal'd* by his *Refurrection.*

2. It is an efficient caufe of our rifing with an *identity* of *Body* as He rofe; for we fall not in re-fpect of our Souls, but our Bodies; if therefore the fame Body does not *rife*, the notion of a *Refurrection* is deftroyed. This power and right He has to raife us, is part of that Dominion he receiv'd when He rofe; whereby He be-came *Lord of the Dead as well as the Living*; and He gave a pregnant inftance of it at his *rifing*, when He cauf'd the *Stone* to be remov'd not onely from his own, but from others Sepulchers; for *He had many Bodies of Saints with him.* They had long before flept in the duft, and perhaps were fo far from be-ing *dry bones*, that the queftion might be put, *Can this duft live?* yet were they quickly fafhioned

in

Rom. 14. 9.

in the earth, and built up by vertue of their Masters *breath* to at-
tend him in his *Triumph*.

If our *rising* be later than theirs,
yet it is as sure; for *in him* (says
the Apostle) *shall all be made alive* ;
*He is become the First-fruits of them
that slept* ; Now the First-fruits do
not so go before other Fruits but
that they are in *being*, though not
brought to the same *maturity* ; so
though the *Resurrection of the Dead*
be not ripe, yet it really is *begun*,
becauseChrist is risen. Whatever al-
terations befall us in death, they are
but changes of Figure ; no particle
of us is lost ; the very least *mite* of
our Frame is put into the *Treasury*,
whence it will be one day taken
out and restored. An excellent
privilege Christs Members enjoy,
to be thus quickned by their
Head ! otherwise the benefit of
their

their reconciliation were fmall,
had he not proved their *Life* as
well as their *Sacrifice.* It is a poor
ftopping of the *Plague* to enter the
Gulfe, and not keep it by that
Entrance from fwallowing ; but
to open it that it fhall yield up
its *dead*, and no longer devour
them , here is a *rich Atone-
ment*, All our hopes depend upon
the fuccefs of fuch an Undertaking ; which we have confirmed
to us by the *rifing* of our Lord ;
who has abolifht Death , broken
the *tyranny* of that Oppreffor, and
made it a *Servant* to *convey* us to
Glory.

But this is all upon fuppofition
that we are qualified for his *Mem=
bers* ; then we are raifed by a *Power
inherent* in *us*, whence we receive
the influence of falvation ; if we
are no part of his *Body*, we fhall
how-

however be raifed, but by a power *without us*, the power of a Judge, that will fit over us as Slaves, and pronounce the Sentence of Execution. Therefore the carnal liver can take no pleafure in this word (*Rife*): 'tis like a *Rack* to ftretch his limbs on, and repre-fents to him all his *parts new fet* that they may be fitted for tor*ment. All his joys are plac'd in a life here , which is the *Senfes Por-tion*; but the life of another world cuts him in reflecting on it, as a Curfe that is attended with pain. Would we then make it our inte-reft to rife, let us live like *Children of the Refurrection* , purge out all corrupt humours of *Flefh and Blood*, mortifie our lufts, keep our Souls pure , and our Bodies clean, that when they are quickned, they may be raifed to thofe Heavenly Manfions, where the *Honours* of

M the

the *Place*, the *delights* of *Vision*, and the *cloathing* of *Immortality*, will satisfy our utmost desires, and show us the vanity of this Worlds good that holds us.

3. It has procur'd the Assistance of *Gods Spirit* whereby we are sanctified, and enabled to obtain the Promises of Eternal Life.

Had not Christ *rose*, the *Comforter* had not been sent; indeed the promise of the *Holy Ghost* was made before, but it was shed upon none till after his *Rising*. Then Joh.20.22. we read of his *breathing upon the Apostles*, which showed the Authority He had to bestow it, and the *Gifts* that should afterwards follow upon his Ascension. How necessary the coming of the *Spirit* was, and consequently how great the Advantage of his *Rising*, will appear in this, That thereupon *Ministers* were *impowred*, *Wonders wrought,*

wrought, a *Church gathered*, and the
Word made fo *powerfull* in the hearts
of the hearers, that they were not
able to refift the Doctrine of the
Refurrection, whereof the *Apoftles*
were ordain'd to be *Witneffes*. See
this exemplified in *St. Peters* firft Acts 1.22;
Sermon on that Subject; which the
Spirit accompanied with fuch effi-
cacy, that thofe who heard it
were *pricked to the heart, and the
fame day there were added to them a-
bout three thoufand Souls* : Where by
the way the Temper of thefe *new*
Converts is remarkable ; for it is
faid, *They continued ftedfaftly in the
Apoftles Doctrine and Fellowfhip, and
and in breaking of Bread and in Prayers.*
They were no lovers of Novelty
or Schifm, but clofe adherers to
the Truth, and united together in
Worfhip : A *rich Draught* this!
which *Peter* had figur'd out to
him in a former one, when *he drew*

the Net *to land full of great fifhes;
and for all there were fo many, yet
was not the* Net *broken.*

By the fame *Spirit* Chrift ftill
rules in his *Church* in order to
mens Converfion; whofe work is
to enlighten and convince us by
the *Word*, to prevent us by his
Grace in all our doings; to encline
our wills and further them in
good; without which affiftance
we could never by any natural
ftrength of our own either rightly believe or repent, and fo be
made capable of the Promifes.

I have here given a fhort view
of the *Benefits* of *Chrifts rifing*, which
if we compare with the Vertue of
his Death, we fhall find good
reafon for that *Emphafis* in the A-
poftle--- *Yea rather is rifen again.*

What are the proper effects of
each I have already mention'd:
How *his Death in particular contri=*
butes,

butes, *but more eminently his* Rifing, *to the Saints freedom from Condemnation*, may be eafily collected from what I have faid; fo that I need not handle my *Third Particular*; therefore I fhall now onely in a few words apply this Truth to our felves.

Gods *Juftifying Grace* we read in the former verfe is reftrained to his *Elect*, or which is all one, *his peculiar people that are zealous of Good-works*; the Benefits of *Chrifts dying and rifing* are reftrained likewife to the fame perfons: *For He is become the Author of Salvation to* Heb. 5. 9. *all them that obey him*: Others are excluded from that Purchafe; whence this Point obliges us to a duty of working, that as He died to *Nature*, and rofe again in the *Body*, fo we might *dye to Sin, and live unto* Righteoufnefs, *which is the Souls* Refurrection. The great de-

M 3   fign

fign of his rifing was *to blefs us in*

Acts 3. 26. *turning away every one from his ini-quities* ; which implyes the very nature of his *Blefsing* confifts in the cleanfing of us from fin; as our Tafte of hereafter confifts in being purified. No unclean liver can enter Heaven; for he *wants* the *condition* of Blifs; no nor relifh it (if granted him) becaufe of the *unfutablenefs* of that Glory : For the vaft difproportion which is be-twixt thofe objects that are pure and fpiritual, and fuch a mans de-fires that are filthy and carnal would turn the very Joyes of Heaven into a Punifhment ; fo that either way he is miferable ; in the *Denyal* of Heaven he has *no hope*; in the *Gift no pleafure.* We fee a fanctity of nature is necef-fary to the fruition of Happinefs; and need we motives from fome powerful example to encourage

our

our obedience? I can produce no greater than in my Text; the manner of Chrifts love to us when He *dyed*, and the manner of his acting for us when He *rofe*, are fufficient arguments to quicken us.

If we confider his *love* to us when He dyed, it is the Picture of *ftrength* in *weaknefs*; which could carry him chearfully to fubmit to *Gods wrath*, the *Jews malice*, and *Human frailty*; and worked too his end by that fubmiffion; for he nail'd our fins to the Crofs, when He was nail'd there himfelf, and by death cancell'd our Bond. Such was the vertue of his *Sacrifice*, that it did not require a Second Offering; what is this elfe but a Pattern to our Mortification, that we would *dye to fin*, as He did *for it*, that we need not kill it a Second time?

If we confider the manner of

M 4   his

his *Rifing*, here *ftrength of love* is vifible in the *activity* of the *Conqueror.* He rofe from the *dead* be= fore *day* ; fo He would often rife in his life-time; He lov'd *Early Devotions*, and *Early Conquefts* ; the one to fhow his *fpeed* in *interceding* for us, the other in *comforting.* How is this a Leffon to us for following his fteps, and rifing to a *life of Righteoufnefs* in the very *dawn* of our Time, when the Morn is frefh, and our day begins; that as He made hafte to do us good, fo we might to fit our felves for him. *Youth* is as much *confecrated* to his *fervice*, as the *Morning* was to his *rifing*; if we come late to him, we are unthankful Worfhip= pers; and befides, the feeblenefs of fuch a courfe takes off from the value of the performance.

But his early leaving of the Se= pulcher (wherein the quicknefs of
our

our Redeemer is manifefted) does not fo much inftruct us in duty, as the *perfeetnefs* of his *Refurreetion*, which difcovers the abfolutenefs of his Conqueft. All others that were raifed, dropt agen into their Graves ; had not *life* fo properly as *death reftored* to them ; but *Chrift being raifed from the dead dyes no more* ; *death hath no more dominion over him* : That glorious Body of his has put off mortality, and all figns of it, except wee'l fay the *wound* in his *fide*, and the *prints of the nails* are ; which yet He bears for another ufe, which is this : that whereas before they were *Charaeters* of his *Weaknefs*, they might now be *Trophies* of his *Strength* ; whereas before they were *marks* of the *Enemies Vietory*, they might now prove *marks* of his *own*. With the like ftrength of Perfeetion fhould we live to him ; fo quit the *deadnefs*

of

of *corrupt nature* , as never to admit its return; infuse such a Soul into our Good works, that may make them vigorous and lasting. Thus we shall copy out his Death and Life in our selves, and bring that comfort home, Who is he that condemns? To think salvation for us is so wrought that we need not work it out our selves, is miserably to delude our expectation, since all those glorious effects which issue from his *Dying and Rising*, are appointed to be *Mercies* to the *doers*, but Wonders onely to *lookers on.* Let us then *put off the Old man* with his deeds, and keep up the memory of our Master in the Newness of our lives, that *when our Earthly Tabernacle is dissolv'd, we may have a Building of God not made with hands, eternal in the Heavens.*

F I N I S.

Books printed for and fold by *Richard Chifwell*.

F O L I O.

Speed's Maps and Geography of *Great Britain* and *Ireland*, and of Foreign Parts.

Dr. *Cave*'s Lives of the Primitive Fathers.

Dr. *Cary*'s Chronological Account of Ancient Time.

Wanly's Wonders of the Little World, or Hiftory of Man.

Sir *Tho. Herbert*'s Travels into *Perfia, &c.*

Holyoak's large Dictionary. Latin and Englifh.

Sir *Ric. Baker*'s Chronicle of *England*,

Caufin's Holy Court.

Wilfon's compleat Chriftian Dictionary.

Bifhop *Wilkin*'s Real Character,or Philofophical Language.

Pharmacopæia Regalis Collegii Medicorum. Londinenfis.

Judge *Jone*'s Reports of Cafes in Common-Law.

Judge *Vaughan*'s Reports of Cafes in Common-Law.

Cave Tabulæ Ecclefiafticorum Scriptorum.

Hobb's Leviathan.

Lord *Bacon*'s Advancement of Learning,

Bifhop *Taylor*'s Sermons.

Sir *Will. Dugdale*'s Baronage of *England* in 2 Vol.

Raranelli Bibliotheca Theologica 3 Vol.

Q U A R T O.

THe feveral Informations exhibited to the Committee appointed by Parliament to inquire into the burning of *London*, 1667.

Godwin's Roman Antiquities.

Dr. *Littleton*'s Dictionary.

Bifhop *Nicholfon* on the Church Catechifm.

The

Books *sold by* Richard Chifwel.

The Compleat Clark.
Dr. *Pierce* on Gods Decrees.
Hiftory of the late Wars of *New-England.*
Dr. *Outram de Sacrificiis.*
Bifhop *Taylor's* Difwafive from Popery.
Gariffolius de Chrifto Mediatori,
Corpus Confeffionum Fidei.
Spanhemii Dubia Evangelica 2 Vol.
Dr *Gibb's* Sermons.
Parkeri Difputationes de Deo.
Caryl on *Job* compleat, 12 parts.
Defcription and Hiftory of the Future State of *Europe,* 1 *s.*
Fowler's Defence of the Defign of Chriftianity againft
   John Bunyan, 1 *s.*
Lyford's Difcovery of Errors and Herefies of the Times, 4 *s.*
Dr. *Sherlock's* Vifitation Sermon at *Warrington,* 1659. 6 *d.*
Dr. *Weft's* Affize-Sermon at *Dorchefter,* 1671. 6 *d.*
Mr. *Dobfon's* Sermon at Lady *Farmers* Funeral, 1670. 8 *d.*
Directions for Improvement of Barren Land, 6 *d.*
Culverwel's Difcourfe of the Light of Nature, 3 *s.* 6 *d.*
Dr. *Meric Cafaubon's* Letter to Dr. *Du Moulin,* about Ex-
   perimental Philofophy, 6 *d.*
Lord *Hollis's* Relation of the Unjuft Accufation of certain
   French Gentlemen charged with a Robery, 1671. 6 *d.*
The Magiftrates Authority afferted, in a Sermon by *James*
   Pafton.

OCTAVO.

Conold's Notion of Schifm according to the Antients with
   Reflections on Mr. *Hales.*
The Pofing of the Parts.
Elborow's Rationale upon the Englifh Service.
Burnets Vindication of the Ordination of the Church of
   England.
Winchefter Phrafes.   *Wilkin's*

Books sold by Richard Chiswel.

Wilkin's Natural Religion.

Hardcastle's Chriftian Geography and Arithmetick.

Afhton's Apology for the Honours and Revenues of the Clergy.

Lord *Hollis*'s Vindication of the Judicature of the Houfe of Peers in the cafe of *Skinner*.

———Jurifdiction of the Houfe of Peers in cafe of Appeals.

———Jurifdiction of the Houfe of Peers in cafe of Impofitions.

———Letter about the Bifhops Vote in Capital Cafes.

Xenophontis Cyropædia. Gr. Lat.

Duporti Verfio Pfalmorum Græca.

Grews Idea of Philological Hiftory continued on Roots.

Spaniards Confpiracy againft the State of *Venice*.

Batei Elenchus motuum nuperorum in Anglia.

Brown's Religio Medici.

Several Tracts of Mr. *Hales* of *Eton*.

Bifhop *Sanderfon*'s Life.

Dr. *Tillotfons* Rule of Faith.

Gregorii Etymologicon Parvum.

Pafforis Grammatica Græ. Novi Teftimenti, 4 s.

Roffei Gnomologicon Poeticum.

Gouge's word to Saints and Sinners.

Dr. *Simpfon*'s Chymical Anatomy of the *Yorkfhire* Spaws; with a Difcourfe of the Original of Hot-Springs and other Fountains; and a Vindication of Chymical Phyfick, 3 s.

———His Hyrological Effays; with an Account of the Allom-works at *Whitby*, and fome Obfervations about the Jaundice. 1 s. 6 d.

Dr. *Cox*'s Difcourfe of the Intereft of the Patient, in reference to Phyfick and Phyficians, and Detection of the Abufes practifed by the Apothecaries. 1 s. 6 d.

Organon

Books *sold by* Richard Chifwel.

Organon Salutis : Or an Inftrument to cleanfe the Sto-
mach : with divers New Experiments of the Vertue of
Tobacco and Coffee : To which is prefixed a Preface
of Sir *Henry Blunt.* 1 *s.*
Ariftotle's Problems.
Dr. *Cave*'s Primitive Chriftianity, in three parts.
A Difcourfe of the Nature, Ends, and Difference of the
two Covenants, 1672. 2 *s.*
Ignatius Fuller's Sermons of Peace and Holinefs, 1672.
1 *s. 6 d.*
Lipfius's Difcourfe of Conftancy. 2 *s. 6 d.*
Willis Anglicifms Latiniz'd. 3 *s. 6 d.*
Buckler of State and Juftice againft *France*'s Defign of
Univerfal Monarchy, 1673.
A Free Conference touching the Prefent State of *England*
at home and abroad, in order to the defigns of *France*,
1673. 1 *s.*
Bifhop *Taylor* of Confirmation. 1 *s. 6 d.*
Myftery of Jefuitifm, third and fourth part. 2 *s. 6 d.*
Sanderfon Judicium Academ. Oxonienf. de Solenni Liga. 6 *d.*
Dr. *Samways* Unreafonablenefs of the Romanifts. 1 *s. 6 d.*
Record of Urins. 1 *s.*
Dr. *Afhton*'s Cafes of Scandal and Perfecution. 1674. 1 *s.*

DUODECIMO.

F*Arnabii Index Rhetoricus.*
Ciceronis Orationes felectæ.
Hodders Arithmetick.
Horatius Minellii.
Sands Ovids Metamorphofis.
Grotius de Veritate Religionis Chriftianæ.
Bifhop *Hacket*'s Chriftian Confolations.

VICE-

Books *fold by* Richard Chifwel.

VICESIMO QUARTO.

L *Ucius Florus.* Lat.——
,——Id. Truth. 19°
Crums of Comfort.
Valentine's Devotions.
Guide to Heaven.

Books *lately printed.*

G *Uillim*'s Difplay of Herauldry with large Additions.
Dr. *Burnet*'s Hiftory of the Reformation of t ;
Church of *England. folio.*
Dr. *Burlace*'s Hiftory of the *Irifh* Rebellion.
Herodoti Hiftoria. Græ. Lat. fol.
Mr. *John Jenifon*'s Additional Narrative about the Plot.
Cole's Latin and Englifh Dictionary with large Additions,
1679.
William's Sermon before the Lord Mayor, *Octob.* 12. 79.
——Hiftory of the Gunpowder Treafon.
——Impartial Confideration of the Speeches of the Five
Jefuits executed for Treafon. *fol.*
Relation of the Maffacre of the Proteftants in *France.*
Tryals of the Regicides. 8°
Dangerfield's Narrative of the Pretended Presbyterian
Plot.
Mr. *James Brome*'s Two Faft Sermons. The Famine of the
Word threatned to Ifrael, and Gods call to weeping
and mourning.
Account of the Publick Affairs in *Ireland* fince the difco-
of the late Plot.
Dr. *Jane*'s Faft Sermon before the Houfe of Commons,
April 11. *1679.*   Dr.

Books *fold by* Richard Chifwel.

Dr. *Burnet's* Two Letters written upon the Difcovery of the late Plot. 4to

Decree made at *Rome* 2^d *March*, 1679. condemning fome Opinions of the Jefuits and other Cafuifts. 4to

Mr. *John James* Vifitation Sermon, *April* 9. 1671. 4to

Mr. *John Cave's* Faft Sermon on 30 *Jan.* 1679. 4to

——His Affize Sermon at *Leicefter, July* 31. 1679. 4to

Certain Genuine Remains of the Lord *Bacon* in Arguments Civil, Moral, Natural, Medical, Theological and Bibliographical ; with a large Account of all his Works, by Mr. *Thomas Tenifon.* 8°

Dr. *Puller's* Difcourfe of the Moderation of the *Church* of *England.* 8°

The Original of all the Plots in Chriftendome ; with the Danger and Remedy of Schifm : by Dr. *William Saywell*, Mafter of Jefus Colledge *Cambridge.* 8°

A Difcourfe of Supreme Power and Common Right, by a Perfon of Quality. 8°

Dr. *Edw. Bagfhaw's* Difcourfe upon Select Texts againft the Papift and Socinian. 8°

Books *now in the Prefs.*

Mr. *Rufhworth's* Hiftorical Collections : The fecond Volume. *fol.*

——His large and exact Account of the Tryal of the Earl of *Strafford*, with all the Circumftances preliminary to concomitant with, and fubfequent upon the fame to his death. *fol.*

Remarques relating to the ftate of the Church of the three firft Centuries, wherein are interfperf'd Animadverfions on a Book, called A View of Antiquity : By *J. H.* Written by *A. S.*

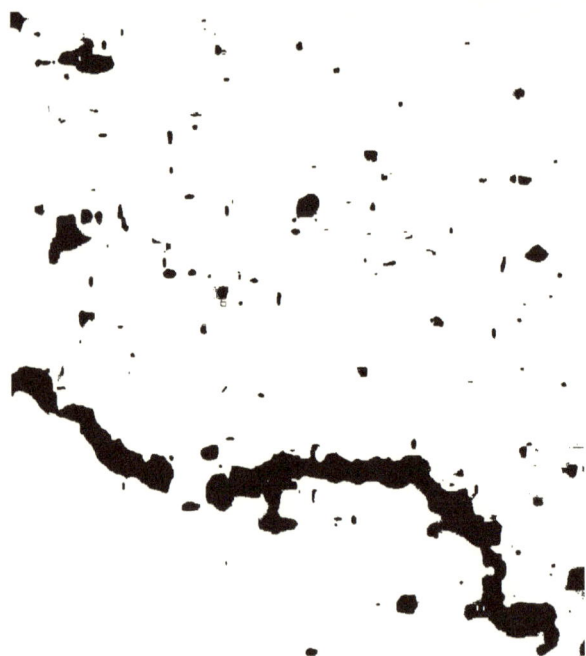